Dear Nel

Opening the Circles of Care

(Letters to Nel Noddings)

Dear Nel

Opening the Circles of Care

(Letters to Nel Noddings)

EDITED BY
Robert Lake

Foreword by David Berliner

Teachers College, Columbia University
New York and London

An excerpt from the poem, "Children of Darkness" (Words and Music by Richard Farina, © 1966 [Renewed] WB Music Corp.) appears on page 105 and is used with permission of Alfred Music Publishing Co., Inc. All rights reserved.

Published by Teachers College Press, 1234 Amsterdam Avenue, New York, NY 10027

Library of Congress Cataloging-in-Publication Data

Dear Nel : opening the circles of care (letters to Nel Noddings) / edited by Robert
  Lake ; foreword by Maxine Greene.
      p. cm.
  Includes bibliographical references and index.
  ISBN 978-0-8077-5298-2 (pbk. : alk. paper)
      1. Moral education. 2. Education–Philosophy. 3. Caring. 4. Noddings, Nel–
  Influence. I. Lake, Robert (Robert Lewis), 1951–
  LC268.D34 2012
  370.11'4–dc23   2011044093

ISBN 978-0-8077-5298-2 (paper)

Printed on acid-free paper
Manufactured in the United States of America

19   18   17   16   15   14   13   12   8   7   6   5   4   3   2   1

Contents

Foreword:
A Thank You Card to Nel

I spent a good deal of my professional life studying classroom teaching. Observing in classrooms helped me to develop an understanding of the complexity of the cognitive and emotional work done by teachers. Observation and analyses are the basis of the enormous respect I have for teachers and their practice. So it is not hard to understand the respect I have for Nel. Her background as a classroom teacher infuses her philosophical writing. Her roots show, so to speak, and this makes her special in the world of educational philosophy. Unlike some of her colleagues, she seems to regularly have classrooms and teachers in mind as she thinks about the educational issues that are of interest to her.

Like other educators, I had read her most influential philosophical work on caring relationships, and I admired the sharp analytic skills she brought to understanding the difference between phony and genuine regard for another. More administrators and teachers need to read Nel's work on caring because more of the relationships between administrators and teachers, and between teachers and their students, seem, on reflection, to be *uncaring*. In this age of widespread criticism of the public schools, disdain for the teachers who staff them, and amnesia about the nature of youth, genuine caring between all the parties involved in our schools seems to be in quite short supply.

I was always fascinated by Nel's argument that caring relationships must have within them the enhancement of the other person's competence. *Sympathy, empathy, caring,* and the many other synonyms for the expression of these ordinarily positive feelings are considered to be inadequate if the other, the object of the feelings, is not enhanced by the display of those feelings. As I interpret Nel, the cared-for need to be helped by the caring, or it is not a genuine caring relationship. The implication of her analysis is important in these peculiar times: Politicians and administrators who espouse their caring for education, *without regard for how educators and children are enhanced by their caring,* may well be ruining our public schools! I almost want to shout, "Stop caring! Enough! You are caring us over a cliff!"

But for me, Nel's important work on caring has not been the most influential of her writings. I found much to think about in her book *Educating
for Intelligent Belief or Unbelief.* In the United States we see repeated and escalating conflict between secularists and religious fundamentalists over educational issues. She speaks to this conflict with an authoritative *educational*
voice, one with which John Dewey would surely be sympathetic. Our job as
educators, she says, is not to pick sides in the believer/nonbeliever dispute,
but to ensure that students have the ability to articulate a basis for their beliefs that is reasonable to themselves, if not to others. Nel has wondered how
anything as important as the religious beliefs of a person can be held without
examination. How do you make a claim for being a rational person without
having examined the basis of either your faith or your apostasy? How can
you be a person of faith without ever having challenged and solved for yourself the reasons for your belief in gods, spirits, or nature; in heaven or hell;
in eternity or nothingness; in male-only spiritual guides or in the acceptance
of female spiritual leaders? How can you defend your agnosticism, atheism,
or alternative religious beliefs without having thought deeply and at length
about what is essence and what is not in your system of beliefs? These are
fundamental *educational* issues.

The holding of good thoughts, the ability to engage in rational argument,
and the articulation of persuasive beliefs are all educational concerns. If not a
part of religious training, as too often is the case, such characteristics ought to
be a part of the examination of religiosity in our schools. That may be difficult to do, of course, but that is less persuasive an argument to me than is the
argument that all our youth ought to have a chance, somewhere, to develop
an intelligent system of belief or nonbelief. It is sad that most public schools
resist such curricula, afraid to explore this most human of characteristics in
a rational way, and in a way that could aid our nation in developing a more
tolerant pluralistic society.

Another of the works to which I resonated is her recent book *When School
Reform Goes Wrong.* We agree completely on these issues, and I am so glad
to have her as an ally. She talks quite simply and persuasively about out-of-
school factors that affect schooling, as do I. She and I both understand that
you cannot test your way out of the achievement gaps we see between children in different social classes. The cultural and material circumstances of
some children are highly compatible with schooling, while that is definitely
not true for other children. Assuming that teachers and school systems can
produce the same outcomes for children in such different circumstances may
be a "nice" belief to hold, but it is illogical and harmful if it becomes a national policy. And that is what has happened. A belief in fairy tales, namely,
that everyone will end up equal, became our national policy under the No
Child Left Behind Act (NCLB). Nel rightly skewers those who hold such silly

notions. It seems likely that fairy tales such as seen in NCLB provide a way to avoid confronting many of the economic and social inequities that exist in our society. Nel and I both believe that a reduction in those inequalities would do more to narrow the achievement gap than would the blame-and-shame techniques that make up so much of NCLB. As I write this note to Nel, there is no sign that the Barack Obama administration has read, let alone taken to heart, Nel's highly accessible, straightforward, and eloquent arguments about the failure of NCLB as a reform strategy. That is sad.

In that book and elsewhere, Nel also reminds readers of the narrowing of the curriculum and of thought that inevitably accompanies both high-stakes testing and beliefs in a single set of standards for all students to master. She recognizes, as do psychologists, teachers, and parents, what our politicians and the business community seem not to remember: kids differ enormously in their interests and talents. Why on earth, she asks, would you want everyone to learn calculus or mathematical proofs? Should every student in the United States read *The Red Badge of Courage* or should students read a few different books *of their own choosing* from a broad list of 19th-century American novels? National standards, she notes, could narrow our pool of national talent.

Overly prescriptive standards, I hear her saying, inform us about what an educated or competent person must know and be able to do. But doing that in the ways currently proposed means that we will exclude youth with many of the talents and skills needed to make the society hum. The desire for sameness in educational outcomes, she argues, is a sure way to push many children out of school, as is now well documented under NCLB, a failed program of accountability not yet abandoned by the Obama administration. The 2009 National Assessment of Educational Progress scores in reading and mathematics show unambiguously that gains made in the 6 years after NCLB, 2003–2006, are less than the gains made before NCLB went into effect. This is true even after the nation has added over 2 hours a week to the reading curriculum and an hour and a half more to the math curriculum, school time stolen from other subjects such as social studies, art, music, science, recess, and lunch. But more time spent learning reading and mathematics has *reduced* the rates of gain in both areas, a remarkable testimony about what happens when you force all the children into trying to achieve the same ends and the same levels of achievement.

I thought I detected in this book something missing in Nel's other works: anger! I was glad to see it because it is justified. She knows that the United States can do better. Designing our school system so all children will gain the same outcomes and the same level of achievement is neither a sensible nor a realistic goal for our schools. Caring for students by nurturing their individual talents is a much more sensible and realistic goal. Helping our students to recognize excellence in whatever areas of interest they develop, as well as cultivating in students the desire to take their place as responsible adults in our democracy, are far more important goals for our educational system than getting another few items right on a mostly multiple-choice test.

Thanks, Nel. You have made many of us think a little more deeply about educational issues and you have moved some in our nation a little closer to designing a better system of education for our children.

–David Berliner

Acknowledgments

First of all, I want to thank the 53 people who contributed to this book. I am keenly aware that you had to take time away from other projects, deadlines, family responsibilities, and so many other commitments to write for this project. Many of you have known Nel for many years, and some have only recently met her or read her work, yet all of you have helped render a composite portrait of her life and scholarship that complements not only her writing, but your own scholarship and teaching as well.

I also want to thank Carole Saltz and everyone in every department at Teacher's College Press for your extraordinary vision of publishing that cherishes the things that really matter in education in ways that make a project like this possible. So much of what Nel Noddings writes about is expressed on a daily basis in the culture of Teachers College Press, and it has been wonderful to witness "care" at work in all my encounters with you and your staff for this project.

I also want to thank Maxine Greene for the lovely foreword and for being my muse in many more ways than even you could imagine. I also owe an immense thank you to Lynda Stone, who spent time and money to travel from her home to New Jersey to interview Nel for the Epilogue. I would be remiss if I did not acknowledge and thank four of our graduate assistants, Lacy Prine, Amber Bryan, Quinnell Vasser, and Olivia Howard, for their outstanding help with proofreading and with arranging the book chapters.

Finally, I want to thank Nel Noddings for allowing me to put this book together and for being the kind of mother, teacher, scholar, and friend that inspires all of us be fully human, critical, and caring in these times of rampant cynicism and depersonalization.

Dear Nel

Opening the Circles of Care

(Letters to Nel Noddings)

CHAPTER 1

The Maternal Circle

In one of the letters in this chapter, Barbara Thayer-Bacon observes that Nel's "experiences as a teacher and scholar are seen through the eyes of a mother." The letters in this chapter focus on the ethics of care through the lens of the maternal instinct. These circles of care embrace natural families, students, and the natural and political world in a view of feminism as "the affirmation of all life forms" (Hagan, cited in Digiovanni, 2005, p. 32).

Mom, Can You Help Me with This?

Laurie Noddings Brooks

Mom, can you help me with this problem? Not your typical classroom form of address, but one my mother, Nel Noddings, heard often during my sophomore year in high school when she was my teacher for Hilbert geometry. Following my accidental lead, the whole class was calling "Mom" for help by the end of the first 2 weeks of class. Yes, Hilbert, not Euclidean, geometry! I was fortunate to attend a great high school (Matawan Regional in New Jersey) at a great time for math education in the United States, but best of all, with a great teacher—my own mother.

During the space race, my high school not only offered calculus for advanced placement but also half-year elective courses in abstract and linear algebra, probability and statistics, and special sections of regular courses—like Hilbert geometry. Much of this was the result of the creative forward thinking of my mother, who was given free rein to design courses and curriculum as well as teach. She pioneered a team-teaching approach to Algebra II that allowed students to work at their own pace and attend lectures or take tests on whatever chapter of the text they were working on. As long as you mastered the minimum number of chapters required (and you could take the test as many times as needed), you would receive a passing grade. To receive a higher grade, you needed to master more chapters.

A gifted teacher, my mom taught us not only facts and methods, but also an appreciation for the beauty of mathematics. We learned mathematics as the language of science. We heard and read about the fascinating people who had made mathematics their life's endeavor, from Eratosthenes to Einstein. We learned mathematics as art (the golden mean), history (Archimedes in the bathtub), and literature (*Alice in Wonderland*). We did well on all the standard tests, advanced placement exams, and special math contests, and we had fun doing it! This same enthusiasm and dedication was brought to all the classes Mom taught, from General Math to Advanced Calculus, and never just reserved for the higher-level classes, as is so often the case.

Mom, can you help me with this problem? was heard at home a lot when I was growing up, and later as the opening to many late-night phone calls from me and my siblings as we went on to study mathematics and other things in college and then, in some cases, to teach. When I was 12 or 13, my parents began to seriously expand their family of (at that time) five children by adopting both formally and informally, so that by the time I left home at 19, there were more than a dozen kids of all ages living at home. Math, language, and other topics were frequently presented as dinnertime contests in my family, with the single rule being that the youngest members of the family were always given first shot at the answers.

One of my younger brothers, Eddie, now a junior high physics and science teacher in California, has this to say about Mom's influence on his math education: "She brought home math manipulatives for us to play with. I think that I understood a lot of later math concepts by working with the Cuisenaire rods and other 'toys' that she brought home. I guess what I'm trying to say is that the process of learning was turned into play and that I was allowed to discover math relationships and such on my own."

Brother Jim, a retired middle school principal who is back in the classroom, shares his perspective on our mom:

> There is no doubt that Mom had a tremendous impact shaping my career choice and philosophy as an educator. I can remember pretending to be sick as a little boy because Mom would take me to school with her and let me sit in the back of her high school math classroom just "taking it all in." It was always clear to me that being a teacher was noble, important, and fun. Caring for and nurturing the needs of the whole child was more important than specific content, although Mom's love of content was always apparent as well. I was constantly encouraged to learn and excel, but also to respect the diversity of others' abilities and help them learn as well. I had the pleasure of being an official student in Mom's Matawan High School math program as a 9th-grader, and what a wonderful environment it was for all. My sister Laurie has described the program nicely.

Mom's vision for our shared profession has always been clear and centered around caring for lifelong learners and helping all realize their full potential. It was very reassuring throughout my years as a teacher and principal to know Mom was always there and could be counted on to "make sense," regardless of whatever wave of nonsense might be proposed in the name of educational reform. She is a tremendous advocate for students and teachers. Thank you, Mom, for all you have done for me and for education. Your legacy lives on in all of us. I have retired as a principal but am back teaching because you taught me it is noble, important, and fun. My wife, Carol, is still teaching, and two of our children, Emily and James, teach and share the Nel Noddings fervor as well.

My sister Nancy, who now practices law in Colorado, adds another perspective:

Forget the pure mathematics lessons (at least for some of the younger family members . . . or maybe just those of us on a different wave length . . .); Mom was a teacher of *thought* processes. She helped us understand that we could learn to *problem solve*. We could do this in linear fashion, *or* (ooooh) we could do this in a multiplanar fashion and *really* solve the problem. Remember, I was the dancer/musician/seamstress of the household. I was also the calendar keeper. Mom taught me to become an organized thinker. I was taught to see *relational* equations and affectations. Logic problems, if you will: If this, then that! I was not looking at trees, specifically; I was looking at the whole *forest*. She helped us understand the *whole*, not just the individual pieces—though we got to see each of those along the way.

My lessons with Mom were not of a strictly mathematical analogy. Years later, I recognize that she understood my thinking processes, and I have come to recognize that her teaching style for me was significantly different from that of some of my siblings. Nevertheless, the teaching was *excellent* and the lessons were learned and have lasted through the ages. Whereas my sisters (Laurie and Vicky and perhaps even Chris) learned from abstract and pure formulation and execution of mathematical formulas, I was intrinsically different in my learning. I needed a much more seeable/touchable and less abstract vision to learn my math. Indeed, my mother found that by introducing me to statistical relationships and geometrical relationships as they related to "focus," music, and physics, she could introduce more abstract thinking into my daily realm. How did she know this? How do I know that she knew this? Well, the proof, as they say, is in the pudding. To this very day (I am 55 this summer) the *only* mathematical equations I use or remember are those that my mother shared with me. Now, keep in mind, I am a lawyer. I am constitutional litigating lawyer. During all my teachings from my mother, set the mathematical aside, and recall that the main thrust of teaching I received from my mother was . . . *problem solving.* Teaching is all about creating a sense of self. A sense of self-sufficiency, a sense that one's own thoughts could actually solve one's present needs and issues (or maybe even someone else's). To do that, a teacher must first understand how the child (or adult) thinks; how he or she receives data and communication and stores that data or communication and how he or she then *relates* that information to something that will be used or remembered. My mom—and I must admit I did not understand this while I was a teenager—had the amazing ability to understand, intrinsically, the different learning styles and capabilities of unique individuals. This is her true gift. To engage an individual brain and challenge it, to open it up and ask it to seek more than the ordinary—this is my mother's gift. Take that one step further, and say, unequivocally, that she shared her gift, freely and graciously, with each and every person who chose to receive it (latecomers are welcome) and you will understand the impact of my mother.

Last but not least, youngest sister Vicky, a high school and junior college math teacher, adds the following:

I think I was truly bewitched, maybe had a few mathematical spells cast on me. It was probably the singing of the quadratic formula as a lullaby or maybe learning the phrase 'How I need a drink—alcoholic, of course—after the heavy chapters involving quantum mechanics' to memorize pi to 14 decimal places at an age when I didn't know what half those words meant. I told my mom when I was 4 years old that I wanted to be a math teacher and, no surprise, that is my profession. Being one of the younger children in the family, I did not get to have my mom as my official high school teacher, but she certainly held the job unofficially. I remember one year when I had a confusing teacher in high school—Mom said to just pretend to pay attention and we would work it out when I got home. We studied for the advanced placement calculus course during old movies at a local theater and from across the hall in the middle of the night.

During elementary school I was dragged to math teacher conferences to demonstrate to a room full of teachers how to do problems. I remember then being asked what I was thinking, not just what I was doing. That one idea of, What are you thinking? is central to my teaching. So many times students do problems just to get them done; I try to get them to think about the problems and what skills are necessary to complete the solutions. I was the only child that got my mother as her official graduate advisor. My favorite graduate class at Stanford was a curriculum and instruction class on geometry proofs in which I got to ask the question, "Mom, can you help me with this problem?"

I have now been teaching high school and college mathematics for 28 years and I still call my mother and ask her that same question. A couple of years ago after an enlightening moment in my college algebra class, I told the class that we needed to end early because I needed to call my mother. Of course, they thought I was kidding but by the end of class they were dialing for me. They knew that I needed to share the moment with my mom, and eventually the whole experience ended up as an example in one of her books. My mother truly has been and continues to be my mentor and advisor. How lucky for me and my thousands of students!

How lucky for all of us to have Mom for our mother. Although not all had an opportunity to contribute to this or other of the essays collected in this book, I know they will all agree with the sentiment; so, on behalf of myself and the thirteen other of Mom and Dad's "children" who were present last summer for their 60th wedding anniversary celebration—Lynda Stone, Christine Wallace, Howie, Jim, Bill, Vicky, Ed and Tim Noddings, Steve Thornton, Nancy Lake, Sharon Miller, Cathy Lowe, and Cindy Egner—Mom, thank you for helping us with our problems, big and small!

—Laurie Noddings Brooks

Rocking the Cradle: Rocking the World

Roslyn Arnold

Dear Nel,

There are times in an academic career when one pauses with gratitude for the work of another, thankful that important steps have been taken and pathways created for those coming behind. I met your work on care as I was developing a theory of empathic intelligence, and I felt such gratitude. I was inspired, delighted, and relieved, knowing that an already significant and revered writer, scholar, and theorist had traversed the territory, signposting the powerful and formative effects on children of the kinds of relationships they experience with significant adults. Furthermore, you moved the context well beyond domestic life into the world of public influence and action.

When I first started teaching, I knew that students responded best to a teacher who cared for them and believed in their capabilities, but when a colleague said that was because I was applying my maternal instincts to teaching, it felt like a reprimand. It was as if relying on a soft option of liking students was a poor substitute for professional practice. Were that all one relied on, it would indeed be insufficient, but given children's unerring ability to sense how adults regard them, it is a critical first step in adult-child engagements. Care in professional life is infinitely more complex than merely a positive effect of affection. In educative contexts, it includes setting boundaries, developing tacit abilities, modeling just relationships, and equipping students with the necessary skills and attitudes to participate fully in adult, democratic life. Slowly, under the influence of scholars like you, John Bowlby (1969), Donald Winnicott (1971), Daniel Stern (1985), and others, the formative and educative power of positive relationships has been recognized as fundamental in human development. The work of neuroscientist Antonio Damasio (1994, 2000, 2003) adds welcome scientific research to support claims for this proposition.

When I set out to elaborate my insights into teacher effectiveness, through the concept of empathic intelligence (Arnold, 2005), your work gave me confidence to position inter-/intrarelationships as pivotal to the theory. The quality and depth of your theorizing gave me courage. It was like stumbling upon a source of light on a cold, rainy night. You lit and warmed the landscape. When you began work, care and interrelatedness had not entered mainstream thought as a significant and deeply affecting influence in pedagogy. Positive relationships between teachers and students were understood as desirable but not truly essential. The literature could be found in the text lists of early childhood education courses but not beyond. While there is still much work to be done to partner lifelong learning with lifelong relatedness, you have generated an invaluable heritage. You have gently and persistently rocked the scholarly world.

In education we must look to allied disciplines for insight, direction, and affirmation and critique because we are working with the developing minds of children and young people with unique personalities, aspirations, and backgrounds. The discipline of education has to be cognizant of many aspects of human studies, including psychology, philosophy, linguistics, child studies, psychotherapy, neuroscience, and all their subcategories. It is a constant challenge to identify what makes an exceptional educator, to understand how to create enabling conditions for quality learning, and to ensure that teachers offer richly engaging, educative experiences for young children and students across all ages. Care, given and received, is a gift to the educative enterprise.

Brain-based imaging will soon identify the parts of the brain that light up under the influence of positive relationships, though brain topography alone will not account for the mystery of positive interpersonal engagements or the care that fuels them. We will still need mystics, artists, poets, novelists, and dramatists to symbolize the human condition in complex and plausible ways. Their art inspires us to wonder, and we need that to energize our own enterprise.

When one reads your work, developed over decades and reaching into education in all its spheres, one finds that it is concerned with much more than the nature of care and justice. Its core centers on the nature of inter- and intrasubjective relationships from which grow quality relationships, pedagogy, and morality. Your scholarly preoccupations are highly theorized, but always heartfelt, explorations of issues that are major preoccupations of educators seeking to offer students transformative experiences with formative impact. In that sense, your whole corpus of work is an inspiration and source of strength to educators who find themselves mystified and frustrated to discover that the key elements of a good, true, just, and personally meaningful education are persistently absent in mandated school curricula, although they inform the mission statements of many good schools. In such cases, teachers need to be encouraged to teach beyond the curricula. If one is dispirited by the effort it can take to develop transformative pedagogy in resistant circumstances, your work is compelling and restorative. That's exquisite justice.

How can it be that students are repeatedly distracted from observing, experiencing, and wondering about the worlds they inhabit by the often mindless tasks set by often well-meaning but unimaginative school authorities? How can it be that in a world replete with copious amounts of information readily available at the light touch of a finger, students are still sitting in rows in classrooms waiting for a teacher to roll out some information probably better arranged and presented in an e-format? How can it be that when we know how important relatedness is in affecting students' learning, teachers are not looking closely, deeply, and painstakingly at the quality of their own relationships with their students? Well, possibly it so often is this way because not only does it take courage, inspiration, and an ability to see students as able to succeed at something good, noble, and empowering, it also takes role models and an affirming environment to thrive in professional life. Teachers need their spirits nurtured as much as do students. Scholars like you, who write, introspect, observe, infer, and see the value of care, commitment, hope, and aspiration, give permission to like-minded individuals to contribute in their unique ways to the education profession across all its sectors.

It has taken a long time for the wisdom of private and domestic life to reach the public arena. Like an underground stream that finally has reached its headstream, women who have committed themselves to both private and public spheres of influence have quietly infiltrated the mainstreams of philosophical and educational thought, challenging orthodoxies about what really matters in education with the power of deeply internalized, context-tested theories that survive intense scrutiny because they are highly plausible and work in practice. Along the way, that unstoppable stream has offered passage to both men and women who are aware that the unspoken and ineffable is often the most important element in influencing others, albeit tantalizingly difficult to quantify. Passage along those streams has been enabled by influential, courageous educators and thinkers able to navigate through uncharted waters and willing to share their responsibilities in the knowledge that one day they will need to relinquish the leadership position. Then they will hand over with pride and confidence to those who have been watching and learning. A profound care about the transformative power of education fuels such rites of passage. Then, profoundly significant educators like you will remain beacons of light shining into oceans of possibility.

—Roslyn Arnold

Koans of Care

Barbara Houston

Dear Nel,

In the acknowledgments to *Starting at Home*, you thank an anonymous reviewer who you say responded with "admiration and outrage" (Noddings, 2002, vii) to several early chapters. The words "admiration and outrage" caught my eye because they expressed my own earlier reactions to your writings. Indeed, they still sometimes describe my initial reaction. However, now, when I encounter claims that I think outrageous, I have learned to treat such assertions as Zen koans. But before I elaborate on what I mean by this, let me recount the experiential lesson in caring that prompted this new way of reading you.

Something I have always admired is the way you directly engage the strong objections some critics have to your work. But that is just half of it. The other half is how you meet the critic. Indeed, I believe I first came to really understand what you meant by *caring* when I, your critic, became the recipient of your own caring criticism at a large academic gathering.

At one particular public occasion, I had been assigned the task of critiquing your work and that of another person on the ethics of care. The format (unwisely, I thought) required me to go first, followed by the two of you responding. It is never easy to accept criticism, nor is it easy to hear public criticism of our work, whether the critique has merit or not. But, of course, as philosophers we are expected to be somewhat beyond the usual response to criticism, which William Glaser once described as an explosion in the brain (1984, p. 163), even though, as proceedings at any American Philosophical Association or academic society meeting will show, most of us are not. So, it is not surprising that after my critique, the other author speaking in response declared I had completely, and perhaps deliberately, misread her work. In that large feminist gathering, I sensed that the unspoken feeling of the crowd was that I, the critic, was decidedly uncaring in my treatment of the founding mothers of the new ethics of care.

Then you responded. You also disagreed with my critique, and you answered my criticisms. But the manner in which you entered this intellectual engagement was such that it succeeded in maintaining, and even enhancing, caring relations with me, your critic. True to your ethic, neither the critic nor the relation was to be sacrificed in the name of "righting the record" or "demonstrating the inadequacy of the critique," not even in the name of that most noble and sacrosanct philosophical cause: the pursuit of truth. No, not even in the name of truth (or its deconstruction) would you grant the "correct view" more importance than that given to the person who had "got it wrong." You first acknowledged the legitimate concern motivating my critique, confirming the importance of the worry and, thereby, the good intentions of the person who offered it; only then did you proceed to outline a reasonable response.

It might seem a small thing. It was not. In that setting, at that time and place, in that crowd, it was experienced by me as the wise, and dare I say, judicious, village elder refusing to throw the first stone in what could have become a public stoning. I exaggerate, perhaps, but not in terms of my experience of relief, nor in terms of the depth of understanding I acquired from you and your ethics of care about what constitutes the best way to pursue truth.

Your response to me as a critic showed me what makes it possible for a critic to have second thoughts, showed me a path to learning deeper truths, other truths. When I now encounter passages in your work that I initially find "silly" or that "outrage" me, I have, as I said, learned to treat them like Zen koans, that is, as perplexing items that cannot be solved by rational thinking but that, with sufficient attention of the right kind, will break open our experience to reveal another reality. Following your example of temporarily eschewing justification in order to focus on how one is meeting the other sufficiently loosens justification's gridlock to allow me to notice other persons and attend to whatever else of relevance may be present. This, sometimes, leads me to uncover the deeper roots, fears, and presuppositions of my own belief system. I have learned to recognize that often underneath the outrage something perplexes me, and it is worth looking more deeply to see what exactly this is. For example, in my initial reading of your book *Caring,* when I came across a sentence implying that we have no obligation to care for the starving children in Africa, my urge was to throw the book across the room. I was incensed that someone should deny an obvious obligation. Upon cooler reflection I realized you were drawing a useful distinction between caring *for* and caring *about,* and more to the point, I discovered something about myself, namely, that I wanted to fiercely insist I had an obligation that, in all honesty, I had to admit I never made any effort to meet. Why? The question prompted me to think long and hard about the nature of obligation and the very subtle ways in which we sometimes use ethics as a substitute for action.

More recently, reading *Starting at Home,* I found new outrageous claims, for example, that the unviable fetus has value only to the extent that the mother chooses to be in relation to it (Noddings, 2002, p. 236). My initial reaction was that this claim is obviously false, mistaken, or at least unjustified. However, when I sat with the assertion, I discovered how much my resistance arose from a desire to escape into abstractions, to simplify the problem. Of course, I want the living, and unviable, fetus to have value in itself, yet I can't think what that means in the context of an unwanted, coerced, or dangerous pregnancy. I, someone who thinks she advocates for women's choice, resort to the notion of rights as though rights themselves give value to the woman, the woman's choice, and the unviable fetus. I ignore such questions as what constitutes a self, what are rights, who acknowledges them, what would be involved in enforcing them, what suffering might it entail, or who might suffer the sufferings. This Flight to Rights momentarily simplified the problem and kept at bay the painful recognition that what you say makes sense: "Rights arise as a recognition of the obligation to respond to needs" (p. 35), and rights are, in the end, only as credible as the people who are prepared to accept them. Value, as with obligation, depends upon "the existence of our potential for relation and the dynamic potential for growth in relation" (Noddings, 2003a, p. 86).

These days, when I encounter your outrageous claims, I stay with them rather than metaphorically hurling them across the room. You might say I am learning how to pursue the truth with more care.

–Barbara Houston

Abiding by Care

Megan J. Laverty

Dear Nel,

I have had occasion to meet and correspond with you over the past few years, and although I cannot claim to know you as a friend, colleague, or former teacher, I do feel acquainted with you through your writings. Of your books, I favor the one I read first, *Caring: A Feminine Approach to Ethics and Moral Education*, and the later book *Happiness and Education*. I want to describe the events that led up to my first encounter with *Caring* in 2000, as these provide the context for what I see as your enduring contribution to philosophy and education.

In 1995, I was appointed to the faculty of the philosophy department at the University of Melbourne and assigned to teach undergraduate courses in ethics and feminist philosophy. At the time feminism was booming: Everyone was talking about the ideas of Judith Butler, Luce Irigaray, and Julia Kristeva, and feminist texts were proliferating faster than they could be read. Feminist philosophy was so popular that I found myself teaching it every semester. I divided the course into two parts. The first offered a survey of the history of feminist thought in Europe and the United States. I began with Mary Wollstonecraft and then moved through the different schools of thought: liberal, existential, radical, psychoanalytic, Marxist, and queer theory. The second part focused on ethics of care as offering a distinctly feminine/feminist approach to normative ethics. I assigned texts by Annette Baier, Carol Gilligan, Virginia Held, Irigaray, and Sara Ruddick. I cannot remember whether I was simply unaware of your work at the time or whether I had foolishly dismissed it as a result of professional prejudice and the perception that philosophy of education was not a serious branch of philosophy. In either case, it would take 5 years and a burgeoning interest in education before I would discover your scholarship.

I loved being an aspiring female academic in what we now know to have been feminism's heyday. Everywhere we looked, there was funding for theoretical and empirical research by and about women; advocacy for the representation of women at all levels of the academy; women's studies programs popping up everywhere, and a lively debate about the masculine bias of university culture, curriculum, and pedagogy. Female philosophers were being lauded for theorizing such traditionally taboo topics as embodiment, sexual difference, pregnancy, maternity, domesticity, and pornography. Philosophy graduate students—male and female—were embracing feminist theory as if it were the new Copernican Revolution.

Swept along by this spirit of optimism, I moved to the United States in 2000 to take up a faculty position in education. I began teaching philosophy of education, relying heavily on Steven Cahn's textbook *Classic and Contemporary Readings in the Philosophy of Education* (2007). His anthology contains a selection from *Caring*, and as soon as I read it, I was struck by your systematic and unsentimental analysis of the caring relationship; it positively sparkled. I more than once entertained the thought that you were doing for John Dewey's philosophy what Immanuel Kant had done for Jean-Jacques Rousseau's.

In the years that followed, I read other texts by you. My understanding of care gradually shifted. I had originally conflated care with engrossment, conceiving of it as a form of passive receptivity that one directs toward another. What I realized, however, is that care—as a form of caretaking—is active, creative, and deliberate. Genuine care—whether for an idea, object, place, person, or group—requires us to bring all our imaginative, intellectual, and material resources to bear upon our situatedness. Care demands fortitude, perseverance, courage, and risk.

You exemplify such care in your scholarship as you relentlessly submit your deepest commitments to new, and ever more demanding, challenges. More recently, you have done this by taking up such topics as war, peace, globalization, and religion. Your self-discipline is nowhere more present than in your thoroughly researched and finely tuned article "On Community" (Noddings, 2005e). In that article, you acknowledge our existential longing for community as you caution educators to pursue it with an intelligent awareness of its potentially dark side. In this spirit, you give an overview of the literature—faithfully representing the different theoretical perspectives—as you warn readers of the need to balance both individuality and community. You conclude with the suggestion that women's experience, and the tradition of care in which they and others participate, might be one model for sustaining community in such a way as to avoid its dark side. You represent it as a subtradition, continuous with others, such as religious and minority cultures—all of which invite further study and critique.

Unfortunately, the advent of the 21st century has seen a decline in the examination and articulation of women's experiences and traditions, with fewer researchers investigating overtly feminist questions. I find this development disappointing, but it need not be a cause for alarm. After all, feminism has played a key role in generating such new philosophical movements as multiculturalism, environmentalism, queer studies, and race theory. I do worry, however, that feminism has left the character of mainstream philosophy relatively intact and that it has not made the difference that we all once believed possible. Here is where your work comes in, doing for *care* what Dewey did for *inquiry* and *democracy* by making it part of the philosophical lexicon. Although not alone in this regard, you have certainly taken a leadership role in the theorization and application of an ethics of care. Thanks to you and a few others, introductory philosophy textbooks now include ethics of care, alongside virtue ethics, deontology, and utilitarianism, thereby ensuring its presence in the philosophical tradition that we bequeath to future generations.

Naturally, I find myself wondering about the source of your accomplishments. Sometimes, I attribute it to your interdisciplinary background and preparedness to collaborate with diverse individuals and institutions.

At other times, I attribute it to your willingness to establish the practical implications of an ethics of care for classroom pedagogy, curricular design, school administration, social policy, and international education. Recalling Dewey's attitude to progressive education, I wonder whether your decision to identify care as "femin*ine*" instead of "femin*ist*" played a significant role. I see it as having allowed you to endorse feminine qualities without eschewing either the philosophical tradition or invaluable masculine qualities. Such a synthesis of femininity and masculinity is reflected in your scholarly research and inimitable ability to combine a compassionate regard for others with a penetratingly interrogative mind.

Ultimately, I like to believe that your writings on ethics of care will endure because you practice philosophy as the art of living. That is, you continually seek greater and greater parity between your philosophical commitments and how they are lived out within the context of your own and others' lives. I have been heartened by your care for colleagues and former students. I am amazed at the joyful confidence with which they call upon you for advice, assistance, criticism, and collaboration. They know they can rely on you to harness your time, energy, and intelligence to receive and respond to their calls and emails—as I know you will for this letter and the other letters in this book.

—Megan J. Laverty

An Awareness of Relatedness

Susan Jean Mayer

Neither the engrossment of the one-caring nor the attitude perceived by the cared-for is rational; that is, neither is reasoned. While much of what goes on in caring is rational and carefully thought out, the basic relationship is not, and neither is the awareness of relatedness. (Noddings, 1981, reprinted in Pinar, 1999, p. 48)

Dear Nel Noddings,

I made the trip down to North Carolina from Boston this past fall to hear you speak. I did not know then that I would be invited to write this letter, but I had found your name in footnotes and endnotes enough times that I wanted to get a sense of who you were. I had not read any of your work, only the titles of the books and articles you had written. I knew that you had written a lot about care.

What a delight to hear your fearless and most sensible take on vocational education and on the broader notion of educating for divergent futures at the high school level. Who would speak on such a topic at such a time? Your practical "business as usual" demeanor, coupled with the straightforward logic of your "the emperor has no clothes" argument felt so fresh and real that I found my attention sharpening, even after all the conferencing and the travel.

It was still more of a delight, truth be told, to observe your steady good humor—were your eyes twinkling?—during the pitched wine-and-cheese argument in the lobby later on. I cannot remember what had set off that particular squabble but can quite clearly recall how fun you seemed to find it all and how effortlessly you had seemed to find that sense of fun. How sane, I thought: Who knew such cheer in such circumstances was even possible?

Now that I have read your early article on caring in the *Journal of Curriculum Theorizing*, as well as Bill Pinar's response to it, and am using your book *Philosophy of Education* (Noddings, 1998a) in my spring curriculum theory course, I realize that the substance of your remarks on vocational education that day also had to do with care in the sense you intend. For care, in your mind, entails an utter letting be, of the sort an adolescent comes to desire from a parent. Only from a position that assumes and requires nothing, you say, can one apprehend another in the manner required for care.

Yet, as naturally as parents do, we educators tend to offer to the young the advice and nurture that we had needed as we grew, and perhaps not received in sufficient measure. We may never, ourselves, have been seen as the people we were by the people who taught and who loved us, and all for this very reason. Our educators and our families may have assumed we were people more like themselves or hoped, even, to forge such people.

Whatever we dream, you had said, not every child will long to go to college, and for good reason. Not everyone is necessarily suited to that particular set of challenges and rewards. Further, as a society, we hardly need for everyone to do so. Your numbers were compelling. You spoke from your own experience as a mother of many children, who had pondered what it might mean for each of those children to be happy. College, you said, cannot be the only path a just society offers to dignity, self-sufficiency, and joy.

Bill Pinar, in his response to your early article, had spoken of this way you have of mapping an area by sensitively alternating between reasoned explication and story, with each, in its own way, keeping your deliberative focus in sight and real. At the time, now nearly 30 years ago, Bill was not sure whether it all amounted to a method he wanted to call "feminist." For me, at this juncture, I think it does.

Bill, of course, understood your content as feminine in the sense you develop in your chapter on caring in *Philosophy of Education* (Noddings, 1998a), that is, as a matter that has historically been central to the work of women, rather than as a matter with which only women should be concerned, or as an area of practice within which a woman would naturally and necessarily be superior to a man. As I imagine you recall, Bill drew on the work of Nancy Chodorow to craft one possible explanation for the prior silence of men on this topic and to contextualize the aversion with which many men were likely to greet the topic even then (even now).

As to your method, Bill may have doubted the feminist possibilities of those aspects of your language that owe their bright resilience to the formal logic of analytic philosophy. Yet he seems to have been taken by the "quiet, disarmingly simple" argument that logic framed and even charmed by the lively chemistry you sustained between those quick, sure flights of reason and the precisely rendered tales of "everyday experience" that returned him to "[his] life and the lives of others" (Pinar, 1999, p. 57).

What is striking about Noddings's paper is that she sacrifices neither feeling nor logic. She returns us to that nameless domain that is primal emotion and conceptually unmediated experience, but we do not lose our analytical mode of conveyance.

Over the years, your observant readers will have noticed how the "primal emotion and conceptually unmediated experience" you referenced can only be spoken in story and verse. I specify "observant," as you did not belabor issues of method, but rather started right to work, relying on us to grasp and so grant that it is in caring that we are realized, relying on us to find ourselves and others we knew in your stories.

I agree that in linking our stories with reasoned argument, we enlarge the possibilities of reaching others with our words. I choose to find it encouraging rather than dispiriting that themes I address in my work have been addressed by you, in yours, these many years. It will take more time still and many, many others to turn this technocratic tide. Nevertheless, it does strike me as eerie to hear you speak so clearly, from those many years ago, about critical priorities we need to embrace when, at this moment, it can feel as though we have only moved farther from them.

The intrinsic rewards of caring must also be acknowledged, and persons must be freed of the constraints that now prevent their harvesting of these rewards. In schools, this means a shift away from rule-bound accountability, and from product-oriented evaluation, away from insistence on uniform competencies.

I remind myself, as many these days do, that political realities offer just one take on a greater reality and that political zeitgeists come and go, all of which is clearly true and may account, in part, for your laughter over wine and cheese.

–Susan Jean Mayer

Happiness, Aims, and Hope for Our Future

Jennifer L. Milam

Dearest Nel,

I (we) write to you in the midst of increasing federal mandates for accountability and standardized curriculum, enormous and tragic teacher firings and layoffs across the country, a strikingly hurtful and uninformed neoliberal agenda that sees privatization and "school choice" as "best" practice, and perhaps most sadly, a citizenry that seems complacent (and complicit) in the *under*education of most of our students and the shameful and unquestionably violent (physical, psychological, and emotional) mistreatment of many. Some have called it a "nightmare" (Pinar, 2011) and others have called it a shame (Kozol, 2005)—regardless of what we call it, public education has certainly become something of which we should be less than proud.

I wanted to write to you because, as I witness the failures and hear the rhetoric swirling around us today, I am constantly brought back to your work, *Happiness and Education* (2003b), a brilliantly articulated and compelling volume—one that I have read many times over and have used in my courses for teacher education. It seems much of what you pointed to then rings even truer now—we are lacking a thoughtful, generative, and substantive engagement with the "deepest questions in education" (p. 75). As you predicted, and as I believe, the ruinous outcomes we are living now are the direct and dangerous result of our "simply accepting the state as it is and the system as it is" (p. 76). Perhaps most tragically, we have lost the joy—the happiness—in our teaching, in our learning, and in education. Our students are depressed and sad. Our teachers disenfranchised and belittled. Families, parents, partners, and communities void and stripped of a sensibility and shared vision of better for our children—for our future. In a world where the word *hope* is now commonplace—used to bring about rounds of applause at political rallies or to mock opposing political whims—I believe your work poses the most significant, constructive, and meaningful road map for hope for our future, for education *and,* more important, for true happiness.

I first read your work as a graduate student in a course on the philosophy of education. I recall what a refreshing, feminist voice you brought to the conversation. In the midst of great minds in educational thought you stood out as a shining light—a caring, compassionate advocate for children and a brilliant philosopher, teacher, and woman.

When I became a professor myself, your work helped me to bring very complex ideas about what it means to be deeply intellectual and thoughtful about the purpose and direction of public education. My students, future teachers, clung to the idea of a real, tangible, meaningful conceptualization of happiness—not a pie in the sky, not a word to be taken lightly—but an abiding joyfulness and fulfillment. For the first time, many of them realized that they themselves had never known real happiness in schooling—they, like many of the children today, had not been *cared for* in their years of public education. When pondering what it might look like to "care" in schools, they were suddenly moved to places in their own being they never knew existed.

As I wrapped up my first year as graduate faculty and saw the culmination of 19 students' master's theses, I gave each student a copy of *The Challenge to Care in Schools* (Noddings, 1992). Having completed a yearlong teacher-research study on topics ranging from 1st-graders' articulation of their conceptual understanding of math and language to the impact of scripted behavior management systems on children and schools to what it means for an entire school to pull together to support the success of one child, they realized that caring teachers, compassionate human beings, meant more to children than a curriculum or the state of the school building. What an invaluable lesson they learned through their own careful and conscientious study.

So you see, Nel, your work is invaluable: It asks us to dig deeper within ourselves, to push the boundaries of the system "as it is" and look to what it could be for the sake of children—not "like being on a bus . . . watch[ing] the world go by," but a pleasurable, challenging and comforting experience. You have reminded us, time and again, that "the best homes and schools are happy places" (Noddings, 1992, p. 261)—let us return to this brilliant idea, this simple idea, this delightfully rewarding idea of happiness and the power it has for learning, teaching, and living. Let this idea (re)focus our conversation about education on the aims so that our desperation and disillusionment can be revived as hopefulness. Thank you, Nel, for being what often seems a lonely voice in the sea of mindless chatter, a voice calling (clamoring!) for us to pause, to pay attention, to ponder what is really important in education. For many of us, including myself and my students, you are truly a caring and inspiring teacher.

With gratitude and happiness,

Jennifer

A Caring Tone

William H. Schubert

Dear Nel,

Some might say that we have not interacted—John Dewey (1916; Dewey & Bentley, 1949) preferred the term *transacted*—much over the years. I feel that we have, because reading your writing is a form of transaction. One can

hardly say *transaction* and *reading* in the same breath without thinking of Louise Rosenblatt (1978); she made it clear that reading is a form of transaction
among reader, writer, and text–not to mention context. In any case, transaction in academe often comes from little face-to-face contact (except hasty
greetings in passing at conferences). More meaningful and lasting transac-
tions derive from letters (now, mostly emails) and reading of books and articles of one another. In reading I imagine dialogue with the author. So, in
this letter I want to continue my dialogue with you–in person and imagined
from reading–relating to you some of your positive influences on me.

On November 5–6, 2009, we both addressed a conference at Lake Forest
College in which your keynote was titled *School Reform in a Democratic Spirit.*
In between our presentations, we talked about mutual matters of concern.
I think that was the first time we had had much of a chance to talk since I
presented the Lifetime Achievement Award in Curriculum Studies to you at
the 2000 American Educational Research Association (AERA) meeting in
New Orleans.

Since those events, I have reflected more on your career and influence.
Learning that you had been a high school math teacher, I noted that my
mother was my high school math teacher. I resonate with the way you still
draw insights in your work from your secondary teaching days, as I do from
my sojourn as an elementary teacher. I recall that my decision to teach was
spurred by forays in liberal education at Manchester College, wherein I began to see how the central questions are deeply philosophical. I wanted to
share this with others, hence to teach, and even thought it could be shared
with young children in meaningful ways.

I saw philosophy as an organizing center for what Martha Nussbaum
(1997) calls *cultivating humanity.* In your *Philosophy of Education* (Noddings,
1998a), I glean a similar emphasis. Introducing the book, you write of the
need to study educational problems from a philosophical posture and you
note the need to know about "epistemology . . . philosophy of language, ethics, social or political philosophy, philosophy of science . . . philosophy of
mind and aesthetics" (p. 2). I was reminded of a philosophy of education class
I had as an undergraduate senior that used John Brubacher's (1962) *Modern
Philosophies of Education,* and how Professor Russell Bollinger drew upon it
by asking us to ponder deeply questions of metaphysics, epistemology, and
axiology. Developmentally appropriate for me at that point, I took my quest
to the Philosophy of Education Department at Indiana University; A. Stafford
Clayton's Advanced Philosophy of Education course was entirely based on
Dewey's *Democracy and Education* (1916). This is reminiscent of your (Noddings, 1998a, Chapter 2) emphasis on Dewey's philosophical and educational
thought. Through Dewey, my foray into the classic categories of philosophical questioning became integrated into situational interests in and concerns

for meaning in educational situations. After my master's work, I became an elementary school teacher, and my interest in philosophical questioning became instantiated in questions of what is worthwhile for and with the children I taught. Thus, my interest shifted more toward curriculum theory.

After teaching for 6 years, I had opportunity to pursue doctoral studies at the University of Illinois at Urbana (J. Harlan Shores, Harry Broudy, Myron Atkin, Bernard Spodek, William Connell, Fred Raubinger, Hugh Chandler, Louis Rubin, and others), and my thoughts meandered around what I had learned as a teacher that I might want to share with others who were preparing to be teachers or that I might develop for a dissertation. I concluded that my two most valuable lessons were to refine my philosophical assumptions and to hone my imagination—neither of which should ever be deemed completed—and I wrote about this. In fact, I often thought that the two blend under the label *intuition*—a rather taboo topic at the time.

After beginning my career at the University of Illinois at Chicago, I was so pleased to encounter your book *Awakening the Inner Eye*, which legitimized intuition as a way of knowing in education (Noddings & Shore, 1984). At about the same time, during the furor that followed publication of *A Nation at Risk* (National Commission on Excellence in Education, 1983), I worked with a group of outstanding teachers and graduate students who wanted to do more than lament the bizarre and cruel castigation of teachers in that report. We started the Teacher Lore Project, which was designed to explore the ideas and practices of teachers, giving them opportunity to share their insights, understandings, and stories. One of the first publications on Teacher Lore was facilitated by you and Carol Smith Witherell, who invited me to write about it in *Stories Lives Tell* (Witherell & Noddings, 1991; see Schubert, 1991). This was followed by several dissertations, more publications and presentations, and a book that Bill Ayers and I edited to bring teacher voices to the scholarly table (see Schubert & Ayers, 1992). I have continued to improvise my own narrative inquiry drawing on work by Bill Ayers (2001), Tom Barone (2001), and Ming Fang He (2003; He & Phillion, 2008).

I appreciate your advocacy of caring (Noddings, 1992, 2003a), just as I have recently emphasized love (Schubert, 2009) as a necessary basis for justice. This idea emerged in bold relief for me when I encountered a short speech by Dewey, published in the *New York Times* (Dewey, 1933). He claimed to have visited a Utopian society where his educational philosophy was practiced. Seeing it in action, he almost did not recognize it. Nevertheless, the main contribution I found in this piece was Dewey's recognition that the most sordid culprit opposing practice of his educational ideas is *acquisitiveness*. It has been accentuated continually over the decades in the language of education for competition based on a warrior model that needs to be overcome (Noddings, 1989) by thinking critically about what education should emphasize, such as meaning, edification, imagination, caring, happiness, and peace. Dewey said that the Utopians explained that the greatest necessity is for earthlings to overcome the acquisitive society, which is governed by greed and competitive selfishness. When I advocate love as an antidote to acquisitiveness (Schubert, 2009), imagining more contact with Utopians, I do not see love as frivolous or overly sentimental; rather, I see it as *agape* in the sense in which Martin Luther King, Jr. (1963) characterized the idea in his call for the strength to love. Connections to your challenges to care are obvious, and I am grateful that your sensibility to care has infused educational discourse for a quarter century—a massive contribution to the contextual ethos that now enables more of us to call for loving relationships with others and with the earth, relationships that pave the way to justice by overcoming acquisitiveness. The struggle ahead is long and arduous; nevertheless, you have urged us well to grapple with our beliefs and unbeliefs (Noddings, 1993); set our sights on happiness (Noddings, 2003b); model compassionate families (Noddings, 2002); and work critically, philosophically, and *carefully* toward a world of peace in the spirit of democracy (Noddings, 2006a). This is a curricular course that you have advanced and continue to advance in and out of school.

Thank you for keeping alive the spirit of philosophy in education and for setting a caring tone. It is a key to an intuitive grasp of the stories lives tell. It helps us clarify and add meaning to our belief and our unbelief. It is central to challenging others to care through democratic schooling that addresses the most critical questions of what to teach, to reconstruct social policy reconstructed from exemplars of compassionate home life—struggling toward a world of greater happiness and peace. I look forward to continued transaction with you.

With great appreciation,

Bill

Living and Learning Love

Pauline Sameshima

Dear Nel,

We haven't met yet, but there are so many aspects of home, school, and academia that you have spoken or written about that precisely describe and enlighten my own sentiments. My first exciting introduction to you was through the February 4, 1998, Stanford report written by Kathleen O'Toole about a presentation you had made. Your presentation title was *To Know What Matters to You, Observe Your Actions.* So I'll begin there.

Today is a sunny spring Saturday in Pullman, Washington. The skies are deep cerulean and the rolling hills of the Palouse are covered with that brilliant lime green of new life. In the early morning, I watched my husband play in his last ice hockey game of the season. Noelle, our 9-month-old daughter, was with me. Our older daughters each had soccer commitments, so they went off with teammates. After the game, we went for lunch with close friends and then picked up some groceries. When we returned home, I worked in the garden while my daughter Cameo played with Noelle outside. The air was fresh with daffodils, tulips, and bright purple vinca. I pulled out some effervescent weeds, sprinkled fertilizer around the shrubs and plants, soaked everything well, and then went in to make dinner for the family. I gave the baby a bath, put her to bed, and now, here I am writing. These are my actions. You are right—my day shows me what matters. Hockey is a very big part of our family life. Baby Noelle has yet to grow into the tiny skates she has already inherited! Gardening and cooking are also pleasurable parts of my life as, of course, is writing. I too can describe myself, like you, as "incurably domestic." I agree that there should always be flowers on the table!

Lately, I've been thinking more about the importance of how domesticity affects how I feel. I can honestly say that my self-esteem is raised a notch simply by turning on my mini–food processor. Numerous books suggest spooning homemade baby food into ice cube trays for storage. I feel great elation by not following that advice and simply dropping dollops of pureed baby food on a piece of aluminum foil on a cookie tray and then folding the foil over quickly, as if I'm a hairdresser putting highlights in. I then put the cookie tray in the freezer and when the food has solidified, I put the rounds of broccoli, apple, squash, et cetera, into reclosable plastic bags. Whenever I feel overwhelmed with things, I simply pull open my freezer drawer and look happily at the collection of colorful frozen lumps. There is so much joy and happiness in being a mother and doing things for my family that make me feel productive and caring. Interestingly enough, in the methamphetamine research project that I'm working on, the women in recovery have all suffered through issues of guilt and grief around mothering and goodness in relation to their addictions (see www.womenandmeth.com). I agree with you: Homemaking skills, one of the greatest sources of joy and well-being, should be included in educational goals. Educating the whole child includes learning about personal and family health, as well as examining how we love one another in our various spaces.

Before taking a faculty job at Washington State University, I was a long-time classroom teacher. I used to play the "Chalk Game" with elementary-aged children. Nel, you describe education from the care perspective as having four components: modeling, dialogue, practice, and confirmation (Noddings, 1998a). This game is perfect for practice and confirmation. The class sits knee to knee in a circle. One student is named the "special person." Another person is nominated to be the "It." The It has three pieces of different-colored chalk. It says, "Heads down, hands out." It then distributes the three pieces of chalk. It then says, "Chalk people, stand up." The three people stand up with the chalk hidden in their hands behind their backs. The three people each give a compliment to the special person, making full eye contact. After each compliment, the special person says, "Thank you," again making direct eye contact. After each chalk person has given a compliment, the It says, "Guess who has the blue chalk?" After the guess, if the special person guesses correctly, he or she remains as the special person again. If the guess is incorrect, the person with the blue chalk collects the other two pieces of chalk and the It then becomes the special person. Although the game sounds simplistic, the children always wanted to keep playing. From a teaching perspective, I was originally surprised how difficult it was for children to think of a compliment for a peer. They wanted to play so they could have a chance to be the special person. It was through direct modeling, dialogue, practice, and confirmation, as you say, that students significantly improved their compliment giving, which, frankly, increased student self-confidence and the tone of the class.

One more thing, a revelation about my image of happiness: As a child, living in Johannesburg, I envisioned the perfect world. I believed that this special place of happiness, also known as heaven, had streets that were paved in gold. I could see myself as a street urchin wandering through an iconic Depression-era scene with smokestacks in the distance and vendors selling wares in the marketplace. The world looked like a charcoal drawing cast over with a golden sheen. I was wearing dirty clothes and unlaced boots and walking through the smog-filled city, close to the dirty littered curb. I was looking for shiny gold coins hiding in the gutters. I was not energetic or excited, but quiet and completely alone.

How was this childhood memory (and I am from a very loving family), indelibly imprinted in me? Was it Mark Twain's *The Prince and the Pauper*, Charles Dickens's *Oliver*, or a Grimm Brothers' fairy tale? How did happiness become a dirty, lonely, golden world? Naturally, my image of happiness is different now, but I had to acknowledge my own experiences of happiness to change that notion. I relish the moments of joy that involve being with my family, gardening, cooking, and writing. Ironically, these greatest joys have seemingly little to do with my 23 years of formal education.

Happiness is being with those we love. If schooling systems care about happiness, then we must teach how to love and be loved. We must operate in spaces of integrity, trust, honor, goodness, and transparency. We cannot be scared of love in school. I have an article in the *Journal of Curriculum*

Theorizing in which my dear mentor and friend Carl Leggo and I exchange letters on love. I'd like to end with an excerpt from one of his letters:

> Love's possibilities are inexhaustible. . . . I grow more convinced that we need to narrate love with a creative and pedagogical commitment to love's confusing complexity, labyrinthine dangers, healing efficacy, indefatigable optimism, and inimitable imagination. We need to learn to be, sometimes in stillness, sometimes in bursts of activity, always full of love, always ready to receive the kiss when it is offered. (Sameshima & Leggo, 2010, p. 80)

With gratitude and respect for your work,

Pauline Sameshima

The Primacy of Relation

Shilpi Sinha

Dear Nel,

I first encountered your work *Caring: A Feminine Approach to Ethics and Moral Education* (Noddings, 2003a) as a graduate student studying philosophy and researching the various perspectives found in feminist thought. I had been immersed in the discourse of third-wave feminism, where conceptions of postmodernism and postcolonialism were informing my understanding of gender and what it meant to be an embodied self. Positioned as a second-generation South Asian American female, navigating the tensions of East and West as it culminated in a diasporic body, I found myself gravitating toward writings by theorists such as Judith Butler, Elizabeth Grosz, and Gayatri Chakravorty Spivak, who problematized the coherency of female identity as the starting point for political mobilization and transformation. I had seen around me the oppression that could result when conceptions of women were essentialized, where conceptions of women as the more caring sex and cultivator of relationships too often translated into perpetuating the ideal of self-sacrifice and the norm of living an unfulfilled life. While the theoretical articulations of postmodern and postcolonial thought provided me with a powerful framework from which to name and interrogate that which I saw, I was also left with the nagging sense that something, with reference to the articulation of what I was experiencing, was left incomplete and unexplored. I can best describe this feeling as a longing for an understanding of the possibility of connection to and concern for others in terms that could not be fully co-opted by the terms of self-immolation. Your book *Caring* provided the window through which I glimpsed that possibility.

To have the chance to work with you provided the impetus for me to apply to Teachers College. I was thrilled when I was accepted, and I seized the opportunity to attend your seminars and work with you on my research in philosophy and education. Interacting with you in class, and observing your interactions with others, made clear to me that you lived the ethic of care about which you spoke and wrote. In the language of Parker Palmer, you embodied the "undivided self," where that which you professed and that which you did was integrated in a life-affirming whole (Palmer, 1997). Nel, you left an indelible mark on my very understanding of why and how to teach.

Through my conversations with you, you solidified for me the idea that I had gleaned from your work, that caring was not indicative of the primacy of relationship, where this notion was taken to mean the maintenance of one's involvement with others on the basis of kinship or socially and culturally defined roles or associations at the expense of everything else. Such a focus easily falls prey to the view that the ethic of care is detrimental to women by reinforcing traditional gender roles or resulting in self-sacrificing ways of behaving and acting in the world. However, your words, as found in *Caring*, are worth restating here as a counterpoint. You write,

> An ethic of care is not a life-denying ethic. Even though its source and focus are the other, it is not a dour, dutiful, or cowardly ethic. It finds joy as well as obligation in its relation to the other. . . . In its enactment, in its application, it is energetic, resilient, proud—many options are easily rejected as beneath its vision and demands. But it returns to humility in its recognition of dependence, for if it is energetic, it is also energized by the reciprocal gifts of the cared-for; if things are beneath it and remain beneath it, conditions have helped to maintain its lofty position. It is a proud ethic with a humble and wary heart. (Noddings, 2003a, p. 108)

How these words resonate with me! While not the traditional interpretation of your work, by understanding the ethic of care to be emphasizing relation as opposed to relationship, we are enabled to seriously engage with your claim that it has something in common with the ethics of alterity (otherness) described by Jacques Derrida and Emmanuel Levinas, [where] "both [philosophers] call for the respect of the other *as* other" (Noddings, 1998a, p. 193). Although not coming from the same philosophical tradition that grounds the thought of Derrida and Levinas, the ethic of care can be seen to be aligned in many important ways to the trajectory of relation as described by the two philosophers. The ethic of care is concerned with responding to the other in a way that does not ossify the terms of either singularity or universality, and thus in sustaining our primordial vulnerability to the other, a vulnerability that can be too easily ignored, silenced, or forgotten through our positioning in certain educational structures and adherence to institutional demands.

Such an ethic seems especially appropriate in this day and age when the rhetoric of standards, testing, and accountability pervade the educational landscape. As I teach teachers in training, I encounter over and over again students struggling to express a sense of loss over the broader purposes of education as current institutional expectations and norms are oriented toward a culture of testing. While such expressions of loss are often nascent or inchoate, I sense that their seeds have indeed been sown. Students hunger for a way to make meaning of what they set out to do in terms that cannot be sufficiently encapsulated by any instrumentalist or individualist discourse of education. Nel, your work gives us a language for how to think and talk about education in ways that can honor the vulnerability that makes us human and originally connected to others. An ethic of care helps both teachers and students understand what it might mean to orient themselves to this vulnerability in life-affirming ways. Each day that I am in the university classroom, I am constantly reminded of the truth of your statement that relation is ontologically basic (Noddings, 2003a, p. 4) and of the need to recognize that as educational structures and institutions contribute to stunting or shutting down our capacity for affective response, great moral and ethical costs are incurred upon ourselves and others. I feel profoundly fortunate, Nel, to have been a part of your chain of caring.

Sincerely,

Shilpi Sinha

"With Care"

Barbara Thayer-Bacon

Dear Nel,

You have been the mother to many children, your own, biological and adopted; your children's friends; your students as a high school math teacher; and even your graduate students. You have touched all their lives in deep ways as a result. However, your impact extends way beyond those immediate children and students with whom you've had a direct caring relationship, as there are many more of us who continue to be touched through your writing and your presence at conferences. I was one of those who met you through your work and resonated strongly with what you were saying. Your experiences as a teacher and scholar are seen through the eyes of a mother, and so are mine.

I attended my first Philosophy of Education Society Conference in 1990, 7 months pregnant with my fourth child, Sam, and in the midst of writing my dissertation. I roomed with other graduate students attending the conference and shared meals with them. Funny thing, they all turned out to be students of yours. I remember coming home thinking, I should look up her work. Added to my interest was my discovery of *Women's Ways of Knowing* (Belenky et al., 1997) while working on my dissertation. I tracked down their important influences as I was trying to consider how to bring a woman's perspective to critical thinking theory, which seemed so clearly androcentric while claiming to be neutral, objective, and universal. My following-the-influences trail sent me to Carol Gilligan, Sara Ruddick, and you, and your *Caring*.

I wasn't so interested in care theory in terms of ethics, the lens with which you and Gilligan explored caring, but I was very much interested in caring as it related to knowing and thinking critically. I was deeply moved by your description of the caring relation and the need to be receptive and responsive as well as discerning and generous. Your discussion of "generous thinking" and "receptive rationality" helped me realize the need to bring caring and reasoning together in a description of critical thinking which recognizes that we use many tools to help us reason well: critical thinking, yes, but also our emotions, intuition, and imagination—tools that tend to be associated more with the arts and with women (as well as many indigenous cultures that are not strongly associated with logical/analytical thinking). I called my redescription of critical thinking constructive thinking, in honor of *Women's Ways of Knowing*'s constructive knowers.

I was working on completion of *Transforming Critical Thinking: Thinking Constructively* when I came to spend a semester with you as a visiting scholar at Teachers College, Columbia University. You had just retired from Stanford University and agreed to work for Teachers College for 3 years as a visiting professor, just as I was tenured and qualified for a sabbatical. I spent the summer of 1997 planning to try to spend a year at Stanford with you, only to find you weren't going to be there. Did I want to be in California, near my family, or in New York City, working with you? I chose you! We had a wonderful time there, Nel, my minifamily and I, and we still talk about it fondly. Thank you so much for being willing to sponsor a scholar you barely knew and for giving me the chance to have the three women teachers I wished I had had as a graduate student (Maxine Greene, Jane Roland Martin, and you). You three were my dream team of teachers, and I had the chance to make that dream come true, thanks to you. I loved every minute of the time I spent in your classes watching you teach and all the lunches we had together. I came to New York City for the chance to share my constructive thinking theory with you and to start to work out the relational epistemology needed to support such a theory. Once again, I knew your work does *not* focus on epistemology; however, I knew your relational ontology does help to form the fishing net that I need to weave to help me catch up from our ocean of experience a description of our world based on relationality. I began working on *Relational "(E)pistemologies"* while in New York with you, and I am still working on those ideas in terms of a relational ontology. Your work is still inspiring me and helping me with my own. How can I possibly thank you enough?

I think it is important that you know you have played a significant modeling role for many of us at conferences (and for me in your classroom). Did you know we all love watching you respond to questions and criticisms about your theories and ideas? You are such a wonderful role model of grace and generosity! You listen carefully to the question and check to make sure you have understood it correctly. You say things like "You might have a point there," or "I'll have to think about that more," or "Here's where your suggestion might help out, but here's where it might have problems." I've never heard you say anything close to "I completely disagree with you! You are wrong!" Your approach is welcoming and affirming and a great example of open-mindedness. I don't think I've ever seen you get defensive. I have seen you get angry—but it's a passion that is born out of concern for others.

Don't think the scholars who love your work haven't noticed that you often get assigned rooms for presenting that are too small. We have sat on floors, stood against walls, and spilled into the halls. Don't think we don't notice that you support efforts that to many would seem small, such as agreeing to be the keynote speaker for the Peace Education SIG (Special Interest Group) at AERA or keynoting for the Research on Women and Education SIG's fall conference I hosted in Knoxville, Tennessee, or agreeing to write a foreword for a young scholar's book or a chapter in something someone is putting together as an editor. You stand up for educational issues in important ways that continue to encourage the rest of us to keep on working and asking the hard questions.

I decided at one PES conference in the 1990s that if I ever had the opportunity to give a presidential address at PES, I would title it "With Care," in honor of you and your work, and tease out for the audience how care theory has influenced my own work, and life, in so many ways. When Jim Macmillan was president, he titled his paper "Love and Logic," and one year I noticed that Jim Garrison, one of Macmillan's students much influenced by him, signed his email the same way. I've been signing my email "With care" ever since. When I do, I think of you. Thank you Nel, for all you do!

With care and much love,

—Barbara Thayer-Bacon

EcoJustice Education as an Ethic of Care

Rebecca Martusewicz

Dear Nel,

I accepted this invitation to write a letter to you with deep humility and gratitude for the opportunity. Others contributing to this collection surely have the benefit of deeper personal relationships with you and deeper knowledge of your work. But as a teacher educator for more than 20 years now, how could I resist the chance to comment on what your work has meant to my students and me?

At a particular moment in my career, your work helped give me the courage needed to change the direction of my commitments. I began work in this field in the mid-1980s focused primarily on questions of education and social justice. About 12 years ago, I turned toward questions about the ecological crisis and our responsibilities as educators in the face of species loss; water, air, and soil pollution; destruction of the oceans; and climate change. At about that time I was asked to teach a graduate course in philosophy of education. I assigned your book *The Challenge to Care in Schools* (1992) as one of the primary texts. There, you offer us one of the earliest attempts in philosophy of education to address our ethical responsibilities to care for the natural world.

Teaching the chapter "Caring for Animals, Plants, and the Earth" helped me to take my first tentative steps toward embracing what I had somehow always known, that we have to take seriously other creatures' integrity as living beings as a matter of care for general well-being on this planet. I was so moved by the story of your son's anguished insistence that you help him save the guppies strewn among glass shards after his aquarium smashed to the floor: "Don't you understand? My fish are dying!" (p. 127). That story, the voice of your son shared with such love, shook me right to my core. It helped to awaken me out of a certain sleepy denial that I had been living in for years in which culturally imposed shame about a deep love of the natural world was keeping me silent about the damage being perpetrated on the planet. I began to search used bookstores for old copies of the children's books you mention—*My Friend Flicka, Wind in the Willows, Black Beauty, Beautiful Joe*—practically the only books I read as a child, offered to me by my mother, who knew they would appeal to my heart.

As the chapter develops, you ask the reader to consider what it means to care for the environment by involving students in direct hands-on projects in their communities: "Just as they should participate in care of the young, aged, and disabled, so they should contribute to cleaning up streams, planting trees and maintaining gardens in parks and school yards" (p. 136). You ask what it means to address such issues with "people living in depressed areas." What an important leap, insisting that middle-class students living in material abundance be asked to consider the effects that their lifestyles might have on "the lives of others," calling for "a more careful and conservative way of life" (p. 137). I remember discussing this passage with my mostly White middle-class students, practicing teachers from the suburbs of Detroit. What could it mean to consider all these issues as we work to understand the history of that city and the damages now being suffered by folks there? While you don't quite link poverty or social inequality with the degradation of the environment as part of the same cultural foundations, the fact that you raise the question of oppression in this chapter pushed us into considering what the connections might be. That was a lively discussion, the start of many more in my relationship with students as I began to seriously move my work into an ecojustice analysis (Martusewicz & Edmundson, 2005; see also www. ecojusticeeducation.org).

As I look over the work that you've published since *The Challenge to Care,* I am struck by the scope of what you are asking us to consider worthy of our care and the complexity of what it means to care. I am also aware of some important and curious silences. Taking seriously your statement that we need to learn how to care for those we may disagree with, I want to offer some thoughts about where we differ.

So let me begin as carefully as I can by inviting you into some of my thoughts on what it means to engage an ethic of care. I work from within a framework that understands humans as living embedded within a larger ecological system. While Western science in the past 50 years or so has tended toward a more managerial conception, *ecology* comes from the Greek *oikos,* meaning "home." Thus, to care in the ecological sense is to recognize the living world as something to be cherished as our home. I love the work you have done on the home and household in your books *Critical Lessons* (Noddings, 2006a) and *Happiness and Education* (Noddings, 2003a). If opened up or pushed out, there could be really interesting connections between these thoughtful essays on house and home and your interest in the natural world. The work you've done on "place" is also highly relevant. How does the focus of an ethics of care shift if these areas of inquiry are integrated conceptually?

When we begin from a deep understanding of ecosystems as the places where we "dwell," as many Indigenous peoples do (Apffel-Marglin, 1998; Esteva & Prakash, 1998), it becomes possible to see the ways Western Eurocentric intellectual traditions tend to categorize, dichotomize, and hierarchize our relationships with the more than human world, setting up "reasoning" humans as superior to and thus able to control nonreasoning animals (and those humans defined as more "like" nature or animals). Such ways of thinking position human culture as outside living systems. In this sense, animals and plants are studied as separate from us, to be cared for or stewarded perhaps, but generally for our purposes and use, not in the sense of an essential systemic interdependence. Gregory Bateson writes of this as Western culture's hubris, a critical, even suicidal mistake: "The creature who wins against its environment, destroys itself" (1972, p. 501).

This sensibility is a key part of Indigenous teachings about sustainability (Cajete, 1999; Nelson, 2008). Over the years, I have been advised on more than one occasion that to look to Indigenous cultures for wisdom in these matters is to romanticize them. Surely we do need to be careful about reproducing the racism expressed in notions of the "noble savage." On the other hand, it seems to me that this suggestion—coming as it most often does from White academics—may actually be a current expression of skepticism about the value of other cultures, other people, and other creatures. What does it mean if, in the fear of romanticizing, we exclude these diverse ways of knowing from our quest to understand our own cultural mistakes? Einstein reminded us that we will not realize what needs to change from within the cultural systems creating the problems. So, I wonder what it would mean to seek an ethic of care in the wisdom of those we have been taught to see as "primitive" or "inferior," not as a matter of "going native" but rather as a matter of educating ourselves about the limits of our own cultural assumptions and the richness of our relationships with the more than human world.

I actually learned this first from my mother, who taught me how to listen to and learn from an animal, how to open myself to their specific integrity. I learned it again by spending time in Detroit with people who many in this part of the country tend to believe are just plain "messed up," as some of my students have said. As a community that is at least 85% African American, where the average family lives on $15,000 a year, and where crime rates are among the highest in the country, Detroit is probably not a place where most would seek wisdom. For 50 years this city has been abandoned by an economic system obsessed with profit before life, left behind by expanding highways, growing suburbs, and hyperconsumerism.

And yet I can honestly say that I have learned the most important lessons about care here. I have spent hours and hours learning about what happens when people come together in love and kindness and tenacity, facing down food insecurity by creating gorgeous gardens on abandoned lots, feeding their families and their neighbors. I have witnessed muralists working with poets and musicians and gardeners to offer free classes for kids whose schools are shutting down left and right. I have been with grassroots organizations as they gather teachers and neighborhood folks together to plant trees and create outdoor classrooms. I've witnessed neighbors cross the street to check in on an elder and return to help youngsters harvest greens for their suppers. I have listened as a young Chicano boy delights in telling me all about where the pheasants and coyotes and foxes live in his southwest Detroit neighborhood–how much he hopes for their survival. What brilliance and heart! In all this, what is being learned is what it takes to interact creatively and generously and care-fully with each other, with the land, and with the more than human world to embrace and make community.

This ethic of care is about understanding community writ large, inclusive of all the living relationships needed to keep the planet and ourselves flourishing. This is what many diverse land-based cultures understand, and what connects them to Detroit. I offer these thoughts to you here with respect and in the hope that one day we might sit down and share some of our favorite stories about where care lives. Let me know when you're in the Detroit area again. We'll have a cup of coffee and take a drive!

With sincere gratitude,

Rebecca Martusewicz

P.S. I'd like to thank Gary Schnakenberg and Madhu Suri Prakash for reminding me to "just tell [my] story."

CHAPTER 2

Circles of Teaching

With decades of rich classroom experience, Nel's philosophy of teaching is never disembodied or esoteric. Yet her rendering of "teaching as relational" opens the door to dynamic encounters reminiscent of Freire's (2007) notion of teacher as participant and student as an active agent in her own learning. In this environment, learning is never static but personal and multidimensional in ways that motivate both the "carer and the cared for" to keep questioning and discovering in an ongoing dialogue of relationship. Here is Nel in her own words:

> I do not mean to suggest that the establishment of caring relations will accomplish everything that must be done in education, but these relations provide the foundation for successful pedagogical activity. First, as we listen to our students we gain their trust, and in an on-going relation of care and trust, it is more likely that students will accept what we try to teach. They will not see our efforts as "interference" but, rather, as cooperative work proceeding from the integrity of the relation. Second, as we engage our students in dialogue, we learn about their needs, working habits, interests, and talents. We gain important ideas from them about how to build our lessons and plan for their individual progress. Finally, as we acquire knowledge about our students' needs and realize how much more than the standard curriculum is needed, we are inspired to increase our own competence. (Noddings, 2005b, p. 1)

The letters in this chapter all bear the marks of this description of teaching in wonderfully diverse narratives.

Opening the Door to the
Inner World of the Immigrant Child

Cristina Igoa

Dear Dr. Noddings,

It is an honor to celebrate your vital contributions to the field of education. Your theory of relationships, particularly as discussed in *Caring in*

Education (Noddings, 2005a), resonates deeply with me. Establishing caring relationships is at the very core of my philosophy as a teacher of immigrant children.

Your work beautifully supports a point I have long made, that rigid school policies can create disempowering environments (Igoa, 1995). We need to humanize our classrooms to facilitate the development of second-language literacy, the most self-empowering skill an immigrant child can gain in school.

As an immigrant child myself, I can tell you that there is nothing more painful for a child than a feeling of nonexistence, when you have been up-rooted from your culture and you feel completely alone in school, lost in the thrall of others' expectations. Without a caring relationship with a teacher, many immigrant children feel—and stay—lost.

Allow me to share with you the story of Dennis, for I think it is an apt illustration of how starting with care and trust opens the door to a successful experience for an immigrant child in school. In fact, it was in the course of my work with Dennis that my present approach to teaching immigrant children came about. The CAP model, a series of cultural, academic, and psychological interventions attuned to establishing a caring relationship with the individual child, is described in *The Inner World of the Immigrant Child* (Igoa, 1995).

Some years ago, I had an opportunity to run a center for immigrant children. Dennis showed up that first day, a visibly frightened 12-year-old who came with his family from Mao's China, with no previous exposure to Western culture.

Dennis had already been described to me by his homeroom teacher as having "a problem." He had spent the past school year not speaking to anyone, an eternity for a child. But I knew that this child was not a problem, but a terrified child who, in your vocabulary, felt "not cared for" in school.

I was startled by his American name; it did not fit him. But when I asked him to write his Chinese name, his emphatic *no* revealed to me the force and energy inside him. All that was visible was his discarding of his cultural identity.

I intuited that, in order to reach this locked-up child, I would need to observe him closely and be receptive to his needs and wants. I decided to listen. You might describe this as "engrossment" (Noddings, 2005b).

As children entered the center the first day, I noticed where they in-stinctively gravitated. Dennis chose a corner away from others. Sensing that he needed a safe place to make mistakes without fear of ridicule or shame to speak, I partitioned this corner and it became an area for silent work and privacy.

After 1 hour, Dennis was to return to his regular classroom. But he soon showed up at the door again—four times that first day. It was one of the early ways he demonstrated to me that, in the center, he was experiencing a sense of feeling cared for.

I prepared a curriculum for him for three periods and worked with his other teacher to create a balance of nesting and mainstreaming. I sensed it was important to give him only as much content as he could handle and not rush the process. To maintain the highly structured approach he was used to in his homeland, I looked for ways to help him measure his progress, but to compete academically only with himself for the time being.

Most important was finding ways for Dennis to express his feelings and finding an outlet for him to connect with other children. I showed him how to draw pictures to make a story, then how to put it into a simple filmstrip with music and sound effects. The next morning, instead of his entering the room in his usual serious manner, the door flew open and Dennis exclaimed with an exuberance that finally broke the long silence, "I made a cartoon!"

His stories had themes of feeling very tired and encountering danger, but he always gave himself happy endings. In one filmstrip, he encounters the "staring yellow eyes" of a tiger but finds refuge with a kindly woman. In another, he is chased by a wolf. He runs into a house and shuts the door; then he hears a gunshot and finds that "a man got the wolf." In this filmstrip he reveals his true name, for the first time, writing "Qiu Liang" in Chinese characters alongside his American name. He ends this filmstrip saying, "Thank you, everybody."

The filmstrip process became Dennis's medium of communication and self-expression, and becoming the resident expert among the children gave him confidence. As he taught the other children to make their own filmstrips, Dennis began to develop socially. His classmates were fascinated by the art of his Chinese characters, and he happily drew other children's names at their request.

One week before his graduation from high school, I arrived to find a beautifully designed poster with a message in two languages. In English, it said, "Dennis is Alive." The Chinese characters said, "Qiu Liang is full of energy and curiosity." With the opportunity to feel safe and cared for at the center, his true self had emerged.

Several years later, as part of my doctoral thesis, I sought out Dennis and his classmates to engage in a dual dialogic retrospection process to investigate the symbolism in the filmstrip stories. Dennis—now identifying himself as Qiu Liang—was eager to share with me everything he could not say so long ago, when he did not have the words.

The "staring yellow eyes" of the tiger and the wolf chasing him represented his profound fear at the overwhelming diversity of his new country and the feeling that his native tongue was useless in school. But when he created "The Wolf," he no longer felt so helpless; in the caring environment of the center, he felt empowered to shut the door to keep the wolf at bay. By this time in the center, the feeling of being "different" was no longer a threat; he was ready to enjoy being himself, and expressed this through writing his name in Chinese. He said the various adults who showed up in his stories to help him represented the teacher who "helped him get through."

As our dialogues continued, Qiu Liang went on to college. When we last spoke, he had completed his degree in advertising and worked in a company. He was making plans to marry and to purchase his own apartment. He was energetic, interested in people, well liked, and quite busy in life.

I have taught hundreds of immigrant children since my experience with Dennis/Qiu Liang, but he is always in my heart and mind. In our journey together, we discovered that when a caring teacher is responsive to a child's feelings and needs, it opens the door to the inner world of the immigrant child. The child can be both seen and heard.

You have described how teacher-child relationships provide the foundation for successful pedagogical activity (Noddings, 2005b). Thank you for these heartening words that support all I stand for as a teacher. All of us celebrate your life today.

Warm regards,
Cristina Igoa

Dear Ms. Noddings

Daniel Chard

Dear Nel,

It's been 60 years since we first met in that magical West End experience, and this is a great opportunity for me, as one of your oldest students, to share what has sustained me from West End, in every area of my life—as teacher, parent, and grandparent, no small part being my continuing personal growth. You, a fresh graduate from Montclair State, had the opportunity to teach the same students for 7th and 8th grades (some for 6th, 7th, and 8th grades) because of limited classroom space. We've talked about that unique West End experience many times. The 50th reunion certainly gave more shape to my thinking about West End, as it reinforced the importance of that time for me and for my classmates. At 11 years of age, I had little perspective on what was happening with me; I was busy being a kid. Who could have known how that experience would remain an influence throughout my life, even providing me with the material from which I would evolve as a teacher? Every time I think about West End, I seem to come up with more stuff, more understanding. I think there's much to be taken from West End into today's classroom. (However, let me provide a parenthetical disclaimer up front: I love talking about West End and the 1950s; it's great reference material. But the whole of the 1950s are better left in the photo albums and the newsreels.)

In 1982 I came to your door in California unannounced. I instantly became 11 again, and you and Jim were again Mr. and Mrs. Noddings. I easily tear up just thinking about what happened that day and how I still feel about you and Jim. You were both very patient; I think you sensed that I was working some things through. Then, I knew little of your accomplishments, and you let it stay that way, leaving the focus on me and my need to be validated. We talked about all the West Enders, the personal circumstances that challenged them and their families. I wasn't really surprised at the depth in the conversation both you and Jim had about my fellow students. I was, however, led to understand how much more there was to the West End phenomena, beyond my recollections. You two, only 10 years older than us kids, were much like a big brother and big sister, for many of us the big brother and big sister we didn't have. It wasn't uncommon for several of us to be at your house at once; we lived in the neighborhood, after all, but you never had us think we could be intruding—your door was always open. Visiting you in 1982, 30 years later, was just like 1950—you greeted me with unrestrained warmth and openness. It seemed to come so naturally. Another 20 years passed, with a couple visits, and then the 50th reunion. With that event I found out much more, so many of the special things you did for each of us—the way the West End experience was tailored for each of us. Many of the West Enders offered examples how they were led to look beyond West End, as you introduced them to experiences that enriched and expanded the possibilities for their lives. For me, quite an average and underachieving student, the possibility was engineering. That was a compliment, given that Jim was still in engineering college. That career goal had a friendly face. I did start college in engineering, but along the way saw additional possibilities—as I still do. The engineering possibility wasn't important for me as a goal; rather, it did reflect a beginning in how I would learn to see myself, building a life of expanding possibilities. Our young identities needed help extending our horizons, not so much for the dream as for the sense of self, from which our futures would emerge. With most of us from working-class families, there were few apparent possibilities beyond a job somewhere. The community institutions were locked into valuing conspicuous achievement where only a few could actually distinguish themselves. There was little consideration for how an average life, under the radar, could be heroic.

Life hasn't been a cakewalk for any of us. As Robert Bly said, "You can't learn anything from anyone who hasn't had a shipwreck," and most of us have had a shipwreck or two. Hopefully we've learned something along the way. No matter life's difficulties, West End was a time when things made sense because it was a time when we were acknowledged as individuals and as part of the larger West End family. We may not have processed the simple and profound virtues in place in that 1950s environment, but we knew how we felt, and we knew that at the center was Nel Noddings. West End provided the grounding to experience life, for pursuing satisfying and happy lives. For me particularly, West End helped establish the beginnings for a refuge in myself–to begin to discover my sovereign self–a ground from which I could pursue life, playfully, without risk to my being. There was acceptance outside my family home. I think in many ways, we all experienced that ground on some level, even though most of us wouldn't be able to put it into words. And I think this has been a resource for the West Enders over the years; I've heard it in the conversations, expressed in various ways. What could have been a more important outcome for the West End experiment? Would West End have been more important if one of us had become president of the United States or CEO for a major corporation? Such conspicuous achievement may have been talked about more, but it wouldn't have made West End more important.

Nel, what you brought to West End didn't have to be accompanied by intellect. Had you not become a distinguished educational scholar, West End wouldn't have been less; none of us would now feel like something was missing. However, for me–as a teacher–the sophistication of your writing has been the icing on the cake. You are the ultimate teacher: authentic, with the instincts, the caring, and the unqualified commitment to people, and as a scholar you have given form to your experience and insight. I can't know all the lives you've touched since West End, though I know many people you've influenced, directly and indirectly (and I take full advantage of any opportunity to tell our story, my ego kicking in). As I continue to be impressed with the level of your intellect, I am, at the same time, hoping that you are still taken by the magic of West End. There may be a tendency for an introspective, self-critical teacher to question his or her early performance in the classroom: How could what I did so many years ago be as important as what I'm doing today? I assert that not only was it important, what happened at West End represents what has been largely lost in teaching. Further, I fear that changes in American culture may have made West End largely unknowable from the perspective of contemporary middle-class America. Few teachers are now willing to consider such dedication without a more obvious return. At West End, a natural teacher performed and left a unique and lasting impression on young people, approaching the classroom with no advantage, just a beginning teaching assignment, creating the learning environment from scratch, while making an authentic, honest commitment.

To some, I imagine this description of West End would seem a bit delusional, something remembered with mental editing, happiness being there only in memory. Even if my memory is selective, however, the challenge is still there for teachers to add value to teaching. Teaching, the noblest profession, is limited only by the way we choose to think about it. Nel, you have been the model, the presence, with unqualified acceptance of students; your prerequisite for the teaching endeavor. That, I think, is the simplest version of what happened at West End. It is my privilege to have known your teaching over time, and it is particularly a privilege to have known your authenticity at the beginning. Even now, I see the person that you always were: the consummate teacher, who cares.

Thank you,

Dan Chard

West End Memorial School

Woodbury, New Jersey

7th and 8th grade, 1950–1952

The (Mis)Education of Bilingual Students

Chris Liska Carger

Deaɪ Nel Noddings,

I have never had the pleasure of meeting you and have only seen you from afar at an AERA conference. I was introduced to you through your research about 20 years ago, when I was a doctoral student, by Bill Ayers and Bill Schubert, the "two Bills," as I affectionately called them in my publication on the gift of mentorship. Early on in writing my dissertation, I struggled with the dilemma of including the literature of personal, lived experience in my review of the literature. Intuitively, I recognized that the narratives of students' lives were essential to understanding any recounting of systematic, "scientific" observation and analysis that dissertation research represented. I argued that the narratives written by bilingual individuals informed me of the authentic experiences of bilinguals and the real-life cross-cultural struggles people recounted from their own school days. The education, or should I say miseducation, of bilingual children in one Mexican American family living in urban America was the focus of my narrative research. By drinking deeply of the accounts of the stories of linguistic minorities' school experiences, I felt I could bring issues in bilingual education to life for my readers and for me. I was eventually allowed to use "nonscientifically researched literature" in my review but was told to clearly mark it as a genre of literature versus a research study. I received the clear message that using literature or stories and coming to care deeply about one's study's "subjects" was frowned upon. Apparently I had transgressed some sacred academic borders in my narrative of borders and dreams.

So I remember that I dutifully trudged over to my university library to look for books by this person whom "the Bills" recommended, Nel Noddings. Such a pleasant, almost soothing name, I thought absentmindedly. Maybe her writing would "count" as "real research" for my study. On the dimly lit metal shelves of the University of Illinois at Chicago library, I discovered *Stories Lives Tell* (Witherell & Noddings, 1991) and *The Challenge to Care in Schools* (Noddings, 1992). Imagine how I felt as I read those books, devoured them, I should say. There I discovered the words that grounded my intuition; stories of peoples' lives and caring not only were legitimate components of understanding education, they were also essential and critical intellectual constructs in scholarly analysis. In my own undergraduate teacher "training," no one ever spoke about caring unless it was in a very detached way when referred to as part of the "affective domain." No one encouraged teachers to think about "interpersonal reasoning," "personal narratives," "attention and response," or "patience and compassion" in their encounters with students. I savored these phrases that leapt from the pages of your books, reveled in a new lexicon that gave form and structure and legitimacy to my intuitions. "Kindred spirits," I thought, even having lived in New Jersey where we both loved kids and pets.

I think that my belief in the importance of caring came naturally to me, almost feeling like it was DNA based. But the climate of social activism of the 1960s and 1970s was fertile soil for such as us. My Catholic education that has been caricatured and vilified in recent years was the seedbed of liberal, idealistic young men and women, inspired by the vitality of a church opening wide the windows of change in an era of natural social empathy. Teaching was not a job, I was taught, not a profession, but a vocation, working in everyday life situations toward the goal of equality and justice. We studied the radical caring of Dorothy Day and the radical justice of the Berrigan brothers. War raged all around us, abroad in Vietnam and at home in Chicago, Madison, and at Kent State. King, Evers, Kennedy—heroes fell. Even as high school students, we were on the fringes of the antiwar movement, staging our own Moratorium Day; wearing black armbands, to the dismay of our administrators, seeing faces of student radicals we would someday see in Congress and even before my eyes as teacher, mentor, and eventually as friend. The lived experience of those days was the education of the time, although we did not have the benefit of your wisdom to understand and articulate how and why the curriculum of life eclipsed the traditional education of the classroom.

As I pored over your work, my personal experiences of real people who embodied "engaging in the activities of care in order to develop the capacity for attentive love" (Witherell & Noddings, 1991, p. 165) emerged from the pages. I recognized in your words caregivers in my life who modeled attitudes and dispositions of caring, although the reality of them as people could not be captured by constructs of attitudes and dispositions. They were Mr. and Mrs., sister and brother, father and friend. They were teachers who greatly affected my life outside the classroom walls, who engaged in activities of caring and embodied the essence of the "capacity for attentive love."

I did not have particularly good experiences of caring growing up in my family, but I certainly experienced caring relations from educators who maintained caring attitudes for me over time. From high school to graduate school, I had teachers who went above and beyond what their jobs required. They took a great interest in a shy, quiet daughter of blue-collar workers; they cared about me. An elderly nun came to my home and told my parents that I needed an opportunity to go to a good college; working as a clerk in the local department store was not my destiny, as they had hoped. A young nun challenged the high school administration, in defending an article I wrote for the school newspaper about the murders at Kent State. This was an early experience of the power of the written word for me and of the need for courage to accomplish truth. Another nun pointed me toward master's-level work when I didn't even know what a master's degree was. They were not the caricatures of late-night comics. Upon my graduating from college, a Marist brother entered my name in a scholarship competition for a master's degree in a new area called bilingual education. His actions facilitated a full scholarship for my MA in bilingual education, which became a focus of my career. And years later, two men named Bill encouraged me to write and publish, becoming attentive mentors as I entered the professoriate. Recently, as I was recovering from open heart surgery, Bill Schubert again took my hand, this time walking up and down the hospital halls with me as I struggled to regain my strength. These wonderful models of caring educators made me want to do the same for my own students throughout the years. "Occasions of caring" (Noddings, 1992, p. 168) have emerged in my own teaching experiences, which I believe I could capture, in part, because of the caring and support that nurtured me and helped form the basis of my teaching philosophy.

Just recently, I had an experience regarding an occasion of the absence of caring that I would like to share with you because your work helped me to reflect upon it with my college students. In a program I've directed for a dozen years, I bring preservice elementary education teachers into primary classrooms where bilingual and monolingual children are taught. The college students read picture books to the children, play vocabulary games, and facilitate an art project related to the theme of the picture book. After one of our school visits, a child left her mobile that she made linked to a book on birds that we connected to 1st-graders' science curriculum. I asked in English and Spanish if anyone had left the mobile, which lay unclaimed on a table.

No one spoke up, so I went to the adjoining room, which had mixed with the room where I found the project. I asked again if anyone had left a mobile behind. Before the children could respond, the classroom teacher answered, "Oh no, that doesn't belong to anyone here because that's done very nicely, and we don't have any good artists here." From her tone and posture, I think it seemed to her to be a teachable moment. Upon hearing her, my mouth dropped and I turned around, mobile in hand, and left.

I struggle with moments like that. I am a guest in a school that has allowed me to bring emergent teachers for field experiences, and I feel I have led them into a contaminated site. I feel sad for the 1st-graders who have just been told that their work is inferior and that they aren't artists. I am sorry that some of my preservice teachers witnessed the incident, for they come into schools full of hope and ideals, and through my program, they experienced the antithesis of what I had hoped they would see. I also feel conflicted because I don't believe that I have the right to admonish a veteran teacher in a school where I hold no formal position. I always feel I should say something; I am not proud that I was silent. In this situation, at the end of the school day, at least the bustling activity in the room prevented some students from hearing their teacher's remark. I found myself thinking that, almost 20 years ago, you commented on the "crisis of caring" in American schools. I imagine that crisis is even easier to see these days as teachers are pushed to teach discrete, standards-driven skills, and caring seems to center on curriculum coverage versus children.

Where I do speak up about the crisis of caring vignette I just recounted is in my own college classroom. It was a powerful, teachable moment for me. While discussing the incident, one of my preservice teachers commented, "I wonder if that's why my first-graders always tell me that they're not artists; maybe she's said that before." We talk about teachers' burnout; we talk about what not to adopt from field experiences; we engage in dialogue about caring. I end up thinking that negative experiences are even more instructive than a positive one, but I still never welcome them and am always taken off guard when I witness one.

There are days when I feel that it would be a lot easier to teach a traditional class in the safety of my own college classroom. Yet after an incident like this teacher's comment to 1st-graders, my belief in the value of service learning is confirmed. Service learning facilitates practice and reflection on caring. I want to impart to my preservice teachers a moral orientation of caring and positive interpersonal reasoning. I do not think that can evolve solely from textbooks and PowerPoints conveying our state learning standards. I believe that education for caring develops best when one is "engaged in the activities of caring, preferably under the loving supervision of an experienced caregiver" (Noddings, 1992, p. 165). So my task, Dr. Noddings, is to be that loving supervisor who actively demonstrates caring, the kind of caring I have myself received from teachers. Thank you for articulating ideas that I see clearly through experiences and can relate best through narratives. Your writing on the cultivation of caring in society and in schools and on the importance of the stories lives tell continues to inspire me.

From one Jersey girl to another, thank you.

Chris Liska Carger

From Skittles to Samosas: A Teacher's Quest for a Caring Classroom

Rachel Lake Chapman

> We should want more from our educational efforts than adequate academic achievement, and we will not achieve even that meager success unless our children believe that they themselves are cared for and learn to care for others. –Nel Noddings (1995, p. 675).

Dear Dr. Noddings:

When I think of your work, the words *refreshing* and *relevant* come to mind. As an elementary school teacher, I am often frustrated when trying to muddle through readings for professional development. I read and reread paragraphs, trying to digest these pie-in-the-sky theories, frustrated that there is so little theory that can be directly applied in the classroom. Your work stands out as something that educators with a heart can latch on to. After all, *caring* is the whole reason I entered this profession . . .

. . . And the lack of caring in the large district in which I was employed as a 1st-year teacher is what nearly caused me to abandon the profession. We were supposed to get motivated by a program called "pay for performance." Basically, our school as well as individual teachers would get more money, not for caring about *students,* but for caring about *test scores.* At every faculty meeting, we were shown graphs of the previous year's achievement test scores, and our administrator admonished us to focus on raising those scores. We were to post sample achievement test questions on the board every day, and when she walked in to our room, the principal should see only instruction tailored to specific test questions.

As a 1st-year teacher, I was torn between caring for the students and pleasing the administration. I had no choice but to motor ahead, leaving students who couldn't catch up in the dust. Students were seemingly apathetic, yet I was certain they were quite capable of performing on these tests. I am ashamed to say I was forced to resort to bribing the students with junk food in an effort to raise their benchmark test score to passing level. A climate of caring was exactly what my students and I cried out for every day, but caring was the very thing we lacked. The numbers game overtook us all, clouding our sense of purpose. I would not care to repeat those 1st years of teaching, but my experience certainly did help to shape my ethical ideal. I found myself longing for that classroom you so eloquently describe as a place "in which students can legitimately act on a rich variety of purposes, in which wonder and curiosity are alive, in which students and teachers live together and grow" (Noddings, 1992, p. 12).

Happily, I was eventually able to experience a school environment that demonstrated the beauty of the climate of caring you describe. This school was in the same district where I had started my career, but teaching there was the difference between night and day. This school was a charter school, started by a woman who was caring personified. She started this charter school by literally knocking on the doors of immigrants in the neighborhood, explaining to them the philosophy of her school, and getting them to sign up. The school's chief aim was to prepare English language learners (5th to 8th grade) for college. To start each day, students and teachers would gather in a large circle to proclaim their chief goal: going to college. As I walked around the school, I could see caring demonstrated in every classroom. It started with the administration and trickled down from there. Parents were even hired to work in the lunchroom, in the office, and as custodial staff.

Instead of math worksheets, there were hands-on math projects. Kids felt valued and cared for, and they cared about their work in turn. I will never forget how 5th-grade students from several countries united in my math classroom to assist a brand-new native Spanish speaker with a geometry project in class. Because he felt valued and cared for, he was able to share answers in Spanish and demonstrated his knowledge to the class and to his teacher.

As I reflect on my time in that amazing, caring environment, another student for whom I had the privilege of caring stands out to me. She was a student from Afghanistan, post 9/11. The day I met her, it was in the large assembly, and I asked her where she was from. Her first response was that she was from Pakistan, as she did not want to admit her true heritage. As I had a conversation with her, I explained that I had a lot of Farsi-speaking friends from Afghanistan and Iran and that I could speak a little Farsi. We made a connection, and she finally admitted that her family was from Afghanistan. She was one of my hardest-working math students, but was terribly behind. In Pakistan, where they had lived for their formative school years, she and her sister used to be hit on the head with a ruler if they did not know their math facts. It was little wonder that math class terrified them.

Because of the climate of caring in that school, I was able to connect with this student and her family. I visited their home and tutored the two sisters frequently. During that first summer after we met, I learned that their mother had left this girl and her sister in the care of their three older, extremely harsh brothers while she traveled. I spent a lot of time checking in on these girls, as I feared for their emotional and physical well-being. In connecting with them, I learned that they had little opportunity to leave the house. That summer, I learned the joys of ordering halal pizza and had a lesson in making spicy samosa turnovers. I took them to see their first film at a movie theater, and they asked to go to McDonald's on the way home. It was 10 o'clock at night, and those two middle school–aged sisters played like toddlers on that McDonaldLand playground.

During the next school year, I tutored these young ladies as often as I could. The gaps in their learning eventually narrowed, and, at present, they have gained the confidence they need to succeed in high school. I have found myself inextricably involved in their lives to this day, and I wouldn't want it any other way.

I'd like to thank you, Dr. Noddings, for devoting your life to showing us the human side of education. It's not about numbers. It's about people. Thank you for reminding us of the importance of connecting with each other. It is only after we make these connections that the real work of teaching can begin.

Sincerely,

Rachel Chapman

Being Here and There with Care

Jim Garrison

Dear Nel,

Over the years, we have had many occasions to chat informally, engage each other as board members of international organizations, and respond to each other's work formally at various meetings. However, I have never adequately thanked you. For me, your work on caring addresses the most important issue of ours or any other epoch while calmly conveying educators to the core of their calling.

Many things came together when I gave my DeGarmo lecture to the Society of Professors of Education a while back. The talk opened by identifying two bold claims you endorse and develop in your now classic book *Caring*. There you declare relations "ontologically basic" and "caring relations as ethically basic" (Noddings, 2003a, p. 3). You begin at great philosophical depth, something most readers overlook. Failing to notice your transactional, reciprocally constitutive concept of relations, they misunderstand your metaphysical and ethical stance. Nor have many fully understood how fully, and effectively, you address the history and contemporary scholarship in ethics. Almost everyone in the Western world assumes we must begin with atomistic individuals; therefore, few comprehend dependent coorigination. At least that is what I see in your work. As a Deweyan transactionalist, I find Louise Rosenblatt's theory of transactional reading attractive. For her, meaning emerges in the creative transaction between the reader and the text. Still, I respect authorial intent, so I have often wondered whether you would like how I read your work. So please let me know what you think of the following sometime.

Your work provides a persuasive and practical response to our most devastating challenge. I am thinking about Friedrich Nietzsche's claim that "God is dead," which for him included God's creator, "Man." It is a rejection of the entirety of the Western ontotheology, or what philosophers commonly call the metaphysics of substance. What happens when we realize there is no ultimate essence (*eidos*), including the human essence, which serves as the ultimate substance (*ousia*) of existence? What if there is no perfect telos (*entelecheia*) that is the essence of our act and is no ultimate cosmic foundation (*arche*). Suppose we did for all essences what Darwin did for species? What if relations truly are ontologically basic? We would find ourselves, as we do, in the existential crisis of late modernity to which postmodernity only contributes a few useful insights, but hardly overcomes. Instead of weeping, we might welcome the news as calling for creative human response requiring our species to work cooperatively with each other, other species, and Mother Earth herself. Said differently, we might begin to creatively *care* for those relations that sustain us. It is very hard work, as every good parent or teacher knows; yet it provides the most convincing motive to live and grow.

I find this response to the existential crisis of late modernity in your references to Martin Heidegger when you remark that the deepest sense of care carries us to the fundamental existential questions: Who am I? What kind of person will I be? How do I live a meaningful life? As you note, "Schools spend more time on the quadratic formula than on any of these existential questions" (Heidegger, 1962, p. 20).

Heidegger uses the term *Dasein* to refer to one "transparent in his own being . . . and which includes inquiring as one of the possibilities of its Being" (p. 27). He is thinking about human beings. *Sein* in German just means "to be" or "to exist"; more ambivalently, *Da* indicates a transactional both "here" and "there" or "at that moment." It conveys a sense of not being simply located in place or time.

Unlike other forms of being such as rocks, plants, and animals, "Dasein exists as a being for which, in its being, that being is itself an *issue*" (p. 458). It is pure potential that "has been thrown abandoned to the 'world,' and falls into it concernfully" (p. 458). His disturbing claim is that human beings enter the world without an identity. We are not born with a mind, a self, innate rationality, innate free will, or innate natural rights. They are all contingent social constructions. He asserts that the being of Dasein is not entirely in its own power. It cannot choose itself from the bottom up:

> The Being of Dasein itself is to be made visible as *care*. This expression too is to be taken as an ontological structural concept. It has nothing to do with "tribulation," "melancholy," or the "cares of life." . . . Dasein when understood *ontologically* is care [*sorge*]. (Heidegger, 1962, pp. 83–84)

Thrown into the world, having no essence, we are the being whose very being is a matter of constant care and concern. Human being is care and discloses itself as such. For Dasein, "Being-in-the-world is essentially care," while "Being-alongside" things and tools is "concern," and "Being with the Dasein-with of Others as we encounter them within-the-world could be taken as *solicitude*" (p. 237). Nothing reveals our character better than what we care about—and how we care.

You remind us that we are not thrown into the world; our mothers give birth to us. You aver: "My very individuality is defined in a set of relations. This is my basic reality" (Noddings, 2003a, p. 51). Elsewhere you state that "the one-caring and the cared-for are reciprocally dependent" (Noddings, 2003a, p. 58). You implicitly identify at least two major flaws in Heidegger's concept of care. First, Dasein is selfish, self-absorbed, and sometimes arrogantly self-assertive in caring only for its self-gratification. Second, he says nothing about the primordial "one-caring" and "one cared-for" relation. The newborn infant as cared-for is unsocialized; hence, it has neither a mind nor self-identity. The infant is not yet a human being in the sense of Dasein. True!

To me, part of your genius lies in locating the origin of ethics in the precognitive, pre-ethical "I must" of natural caring, claiming that even "maternal animals take care of their offspring" (Noddings, 2003a, p. 79). Very few "thinkers" dare to go to such prelinguistic existential depths. At the bottom of being, caregivers hold us in existence, not abstract rational essences. Right relationship binds us to the world. We live by the grace of others. You reveal that we must co-create our essence: we cannot simply discover it.

It is not just that you go so far beyond Heidegger and others in responding with simple good sense to the crisis of modernity; it is also that you respond with a rare analytical acumen too few appreciate. You begin at an existential level that most philosophers, and especially analytical philosophers, fear and then develop your philosophy of care with an analytical exactitude that should appeal to the analytical mind, where it is willing to begin where the problem really resides. I say this as someone who entered education immediately after leaving a National Science Foundation grant in mathematical logic. Unlikely many, I appreciate the fact that you hold an advanced degree in mathematics and know how to think analytically from the assumption that you already know the conclusion and need only find the means for getting there. Astute intuition often precedes conception and penetrates deeper. What do you think of all this?

Whatever you think, let me conclude by saying that your work has meant much to me, even if my response is merely a creative misreading.

Cordially,

Jim Garrison (PAX)

A Curriculum of Critical Compassion

William M. Reynolds

Dear Nel,

I have been reading your work for years. I remember when I was a graduate student at the University of Rochester and reading an essay of yours in the *Journal of Curriculum Theorizing* (Noddings, 1981). It was my initial introduction to your conceptualizations of caring. At the time, I was teaching high school English in upstate New York. Your words about collaborative research and relationships with students made sense to me within the context of public schools as well. "We approach our goal by living with those whom we teach in a caring community, through modeling, dialogue, practice and confirmation" (Noddings, 1986, p. 502). Your writing helped me name my experiences. Teaching in that high school in an economically depressed rural area allowed me to understand the necessity of working with and developing compassionate, empathic relationships with my students. Working with youth in that context was a daily struggle to implement a compassionate practice. It was in the early 1980s and it was the beginnings of competency testing in New York State. For every student there were opportunities to demonstrate empathy and compassion. Of course, those moments were not in the official curriculum. Reflecting and remembering my experiences in high school, I wrote about one incident of the intricate involvement of a curriculum of empathy (Reynolds, 2003).

Ron, a student in a small rural high school, is poor, labeled, and rejected. His mother receives a Social Security check of $300 each month for Ron's disability. His disability could be alleviated by an operation, but his mother refuses to give up the Social Security payment. The operation would end the disability check. The home in which the family lives has no running water and they must carry water from a nearby home. They wash their clothes in the same water in which they wash their dishes–dishes first, clothes second. Ron has one set of clothes. He wears them every day to school. Soon the smell becomes unbearable. One teacher decides to give Ron some clothing to help alleviate the problem. The alleviation scheme becomes elaborate. The home economics teacher, the physical education teacher, the guidance counselor, the special education teacher, and the principal all become in- volved in the effort. Ron arrives in the morning and goes directly to the locker room. Here he takes a shower, leaves the clothes he wears from home, and is provided with clean clothes. Meanwhile his "home clothing" is taken to the home economics room and washed. He spends the day going to class- es, and in the afternoon, just before school lets out, he returns to the locker room and puts on the home clothes. This process continues every day for the rest of the year. At the end of the year Ron is able to venture out into the world, receive a place at a group home, and find a job. A few months later, in an effort to communicate with the teacher who helped him, he writes that teacher a note. It simply says:

> Dear Mr.____
>   Thank you so much for everything you did for me. I will never forget you.
>
> > Your frend [*sic*]
> > Ron (Reynolds, 2003, p. 51).

That experience, among others, and your insightful writing on compas- sionate education are the traces that influence my pedagogy. I continue to develop my pedagogical practice to work within a curriculum of empathy that views pedagogy as a compassionate, empathetic, passionate, critical, complicated conversation. This is not the conventional wisdom at any level of education at the present historical moment, with its emphasis on all things consumptive. "*Becoming a consumer,* then can be interpreted in several ways. In today's schooling, it usually refers to the students' gradual transition from childhood to adult, responsible forms of buying" (Noddings, 2006a, p. 171). As you can see, your work has been a consistent influence on my thinking.

Fast-forward to 2010–I am teaching preservice teachers in a teacher edu- cation program. These students come into the teacher education program with visions of testing, scripted lesson plans and lecturing dancing in their heads. It is their experience of schooling. My course confronts those experi- ences. Imagine my delight when I first read your book *Critical Lessons* (Nod- dings, 2006a). You make the connection, which I believe is crucial when contemplating pedagogy–the connection that a teacher is demonstrating compassion and empathy when she develops a pedagogy that emphasizes critical thinking about the larger socioeconomic, political milieu—a critical pedagogy. "To neglect critical thinking on topics central to everyday life is to make the word *education* virtually meaningless" (Noddings, 2006a, p. 4).

Students entering teacher education programs do not expect, for the most part, to be engaged in compassionate, empathetic, passionate, critical, complicated conversations about issues such as race, class, gender, and sexual preference. They expect PowerPoint presentations. Their initial reaction is that I am a negative person teaching a negative, pessimistic curriculum. I attempt to demonstrate to them that a hopeless curriculum of the memorization of disconnected, discrete bits of information and testing is negative and a critical pedagogy is a pedagogy filled compassion and hope.

I decided in 2010 to enlist your book as part of the required reading list in my undergraduate class—Critical and Contemporary Issues in Education. Along with works by Kozol (2008), McLaren (2007), Ayers (2001), and Steinberg and Kincheloe (1997), it provides the students with an alternative to the contemporary mainstream educational textbook reading. The students are required to read the texts and then we have discussions based upon their readings. They are also required to write reaction papers to the texts. These papers are based on the students' reactions to the texts, not on their summaries of the content. The students are initially confused. They frequently ask me if I am sure I want their thinking and opinions. They have told me that they are not used to writing papers in which they express their thinking. I respond by emphasizing that their thinking is what matters. I have often had the students ask me what I want them to think. This is certainly evidence of a banking education.

I was especially interested in their responses to your text. The discussions and papers that resulted from the reading of your book were astounding. The most passionate discussions centered on the chapter "The Psychology of War." Since many of the students know young men and women or had spouses who were involved in the wars in Iraq and Afghanistan, there was a strong emotional connection with the ideas expressed in the discussions. I had to express to the students that these engaged discussions are what education can be. The other chapter that elicited much discussion was your analysis of religion. Living and teaching in the South leads one to recognize that religion is always an issue that needs much critical discussion. Many of the students are particularly uncomfortable thinking critically about religion. But we managed to engage it. Compassion and critique were necessary in this case.

At the end of the discussions the students turned in their reaction papers. Along with expressing their initial anxiety with the topics and their disagreements, many of the students expressed that they liked the book and that

into the night the previous evening? Whose parents sent her to school in an "embarrassing" shirt and who is still distraught over her appearance? Is it critical for everyone to take that spelling test right now? Can some students take it now and others take it later in the day or next week? Should there be a place in the classroom where students can sit to sort things out, to ponder, to be sad, to nap, to study so the impending assessment is not tainted (made unreliable, in those hard assessment terms) by concerns outside the realm of the classroom and the scope of the assessment? Can we show caring for students by challenging them, holding them accountable for learning and remembering their humanity and the demands of their lives beyond school? We must consider who they are; as you say, "We cannot ignore our children—their purposes, anxieties, and relationships—in the service of making them more competent in academic skills" (2005c, p. 10). Nor can we ignore them because today happens to be "test day," a day more important than other days, a day more important than care.

Thank you, Nel, for articulating so well what I have felt in my teaching and for challenging me to think harder and care more for my students. My students know I care about them and I see with them, as you clearly state, that "the desire to be cared for is almost certainly a universal human characteristic" (2005c, p. 17). I look forward to reading more of your work.

—Marlynn Griffin

What Matters Most

Kathy Hytten

> A large part of every curriculum should be devoted to Life itself . . . and many lessons—not just an odd one here and there—should be wonderful—that is, designed to excite wonder, awe, and appreciation of the world and the place of human beings in it. (Noddings, 2006a, p. 290)

Dear Nel,

It is a real honor to be able to pay some small tribute to you and your large body of work. Your ideas had a great influence on my development as a scholar and philosopher of education well before I ever met you. As my doctoral advisor, Lynda Stone, was one of your doctoral advisees, you were an important part of my graduate school experience, both in the materials I was exposed to and in Lynda's sensibilities as a person and a scholar. I like to believe that some of your influence on her has rubbed off on me too. As a graduate student, I recall first being challenged by your sophisticated philosophical reflections in *Caring: A Feminine Approach to Ethics and Moral Education* (2003a) and then really starting to see how important these reflections were as you imagined them in action in *The Challenge to Care in Schools: An Alternative Approach to Education* (1992). Before graduating, we also tackled *Women and Evil* (1989) and *Educating for Intelligent Belief or Unbelief* (1993). Since then, I have gone on to teach many of your books to my own students, always looking forward to where your mind and passions travel in your newest efforts. There are so many ways in which your ideas have influenced me that it is impossible to address all of them in such a limited space. However, there is one issue you have consistently helped me to foreground in my thinking, that is, the question of the kinds of people we want in the world, as our family members; friends; neighbors; coworkers; and fellow local, national, and global citizens. I so appreciate how you argue that it is this broad question that should drive our thinking about education, not more narrow questions about objectives of lessons, goals of teaching certain topics or subjects, and standards to be achieved by all students.

In all your writing, you remind me of the value of thinking about ultimate aims and purposes, both in education and in life. As you say, to talk about aims is to talk about "the deepest questions in education" (Noddings, 2003b, p. 75). Why do we need universal public education? Why do we teach the subjects we do? Are there better ways to organize schools? What kinds of people should educators help to shape? How should we balance individual passions and interests with the needs of a larger society? What responsibilities do we have toward others, both near and far? In the high-stakes climate of No Child Left Behind, there is depressingly little attention paid to these kinds of questions in our public discourse about education. These deeper questions animate those of us in philosophy of education, but as you so convincingly argue, all of us should be taught how to think critically, to discern the relevant from the irrelevant, to make connections across the spheres of our lives, and to become our best selves: "people with pleasing talents, useful and satisfying occupations, self-understanding, sound character, a host of appreciations, and a commitment to continuous learning" (Noddings, 2003b, p. 23).

Among the many possibilities, three lessons from your work really stand out to me and pervade my own efforts as a teacher, scholar, and person. In so many different ways, sometimes subtle and other times overt, you remind me that I should always strive to be reflective, caring, and happy. As you argue in the beginning of *Critical Lessons: What Our Schools Should Teach*, "Possibly no goal of education is more important—or more neglected—than self-understanding" (Noddings, 2006a, p. 10). I agree that we don't think enough about why we feel and believe what we do, where our beliefs come from, and if and how different ways of thinking might serve us, and those around us, better. Becoming more self-aware also entails understanding our social positionality and how it shapes our life experiences. While I always advocated for the oppressed, it took me quite a while to begin to understand that fighting for the marginalized would never succeed unless I also understood how privilege operates in my life and how to disrupt the systematic privileging of certain groups of people. Whenever I teach Paulo Freire's *Pedagogy of the Oppressed* (2007), I always introduce my students to the corollary need that you articulate so well, for pedagogy for the oppressor (Noddings, 1989, pp. 166–174). Amid pervasive feelings of entitlement and self-indulgence, we could all use more lessons in mediation, moderation, and sharing.

No doubt you are most well-known for your work on caring. I love the way you extend the idea of caring into so many different domains, not only for people both near and far but also for the environment, for things, and even for ideas. In my 14 years as a professor, I have found that it is the relationships I develop with students, especially through dialogue and confirmation, that matter most to them, not the materials I teach them. Even when I feel overwhelmed with work, I try to remind myself to keep my office door open frequently, to be present for students, to genuinely listen to them, and to respond to their needs as best I can. Too often students experience schools and universities as impersonal, unresponsive bureaucracies, not as welcoming communities. I am convinced that changing this reality would go a long way toward creating more "competent, caring, loving and lovable people" (Noddings, 2005c, p. xxvi).

Finally, I love that you devote a whole book to happiness in education. If there is one thing we all want in life, it is to be happy. Of course we each define it somewhat differently, but certainly schools should help us to think about what happiness means in our lives, as well as how to see our own fulfillment tied to the fulfillment of those around us. I totally agree that happy people are rarely violent and cruel, and they tend to give back to their communities, work to bring out the best in others, and care for all that surrounds them. Moreover, they celebrate wonder and joy and have a healthy sense of balance, perspective, playfulness, and humor in their lives. Your work always reminds me that these things matter. I also admire how you model these beliefs in your own life and have always appreciated the conversations we have had over the past two decades. Thank you for helping me to see the world differently, especially with hopefulness, compassion, and generosity.

Best wishes,

Kathy Hytten

Tilting to Care in the Academy

Tricia M. Kress

Dear Nel,

In a recent article in the *Journal of Educational Controversy* (*JEC*) (Kress, 2010), I use the metaphor of a game of pinball to challenge educators to consider the degree to which it is possible for educators to truly be postformal (Thomas & Kincheloe, 2006) and democratic (Greene, 1988) in our pedagogy as we work within social, academic, and ideological structures that regulate our actions, both from without (as in standards, tenure and promotion, policy mandates, etc.) and within (as in our and our students' internalized understandings of hegemonic academic and social norms). I emphasize the need to continually work toward developing *conscientização* (Freire, 2007) to improve our practice and enhance our students' learning. For postformal, democratic educators, teaching in this way entails a process of continually pushing back, or tilting, against the gravitational pull of the ideological boundaries of the "banking" model (Freire, 2007) of education. Tilting is precarious because we must be careful not to push too hard lest we risk shutting down learning, an end result that I refer to as *tilting* the machine. Here, I would like to revisit this notion of tilting and ask you how educators might naturally care within U.S. public education, which is overwhelmingly individualistic, hierarchical, and authoritarian by design (Au, 2010). Perhaps together, we can envision a care in academia (and education more generally) that is tied to hope for a more humane society.

Ethical Care as Humanitarianism

According to your definition (Noddings, 1998b), natural care occurs through dialogue within a relationship of carer and cared-for. In U.S. education, this appears to be a contradiction. Buber's notion of dialogue (on which you draw in your work) is parallel to Freire's work (1981), in which dialogue is reciprocal and occurring within "a horizontal [not vertical] relationship between persons" (p. 45). Yet traditional relationships between teachers and students in U.S. educational institutions cannot commonly be thought of as horizontal no matter how amiable they are, simply because they are embedded within hierarchical structures. As Freire explains, "Closeness of an affective type between persons of different 'social status' does not diminish the distance imposed by and implicit in the 'status'" (p. 120). These status differentials in education are inherited from society and are reified as teachers and students interact within hierarchical educational structures on a daily basis.

While, undoubtedly, some horizontal relationships can and do develop despite these deeply rooted vertical structures, most teacher-student relationships will necessarily be vertical by default, since hierarchies are consistently reinforced through grading, testing, benchmarks, and promotion for students and through standards, evaluation, tenure, and promotion for faculty. Both teachers and students are compelled to climb hierarchical ladders, which is antithetical to Freire's call for teachers to become teacher-students and students to become student-teachers. Consequently, natural caring through dialogue in a Freirean sense is unlikely to emerge within educational structures that are designed to prohibit true dialogue across horizontal relationships. Rather, these structures encourage what Freire refers to as "anti-dialogue," that is, "vertical relationships between persons" in which "the relation of empathy between the 'poles' is broken" (1981, p. 46).

In this regard, can "ethical care" actually be considered care at all, or is it just a gentle means of "manipulating, steering and 'domesticating'" students in an inherently oppressive system (Freire, 1981, p. 116)? When educators extend ethical care out of a sense of moral obligation, they "care" because they experience a sensation of "I must" even though they do not necessarily desire to care. Within the unequal relationship of teacher over student, could ethical care be construed as a form of humanitarianism as defined by Freire (i.e., a more powerful party extends aid while the oppressor-oppressed relationship remains intact)? In a Freirean sense, "care" that allows unequal structures to remain intact would itself become a feature of the oppressive relationship, regardless of the carer's intentions. Oppressive structures such as these inhibit the development of natural caring by preventing true dialogue among equals. This compels educators to frequently draw on ethical caring, while the structures themselves remain unchanged. How might we as educators push back against these antidialogue structures while not sacrificing ourselves and our careers?

Tilting Toward Humanistic Care

As an educator in the academy, I am trapped in this contradiction because by virtue of my profession, I am simultaneously compelled to care and to not care. In your work, you explain that ethical caring results from circumstances when the carer is faced with conflicting feelings of "I must" and "I want not." You do not, however, address what happens in the case of educators like myself who encounter feelings of "I must not" that emerge from working within a hierarchical system that has real consequences for caring. "I must not" often comes into conflict with "I must," which is tied to the very foundation of what it means to be an educator. Simply caring for my students will not enable me to stay in the academy; I must do service (another form of caring), and I must develop scholarship. This third component in particular requires to a great degree that I take on the disposition of "I must not." If I care too deeply and give too much of myself, my scholarly productivity diminishes; I sacrifice myself and my career. If I care too little, my relationships with my students and colleagues and my own sense of ethics are compromised; I sacrifice those I work with and my own beliefs. Tilting to care in the academy is precarious as the gravitational force of antidialogue pulls me always toward the gutter.

You emphasize (Noddings, 2003a) that we cannot care for everyone, because if we try to do so, caring is reduced to mere talk. However, perhaps we can instead think of care as a form of humanism, in which our care for everyone is manifest in our desire for a better world. This means embodying humanistic caring in not only our individual relationships but also our classroom practices, service to the university and community, and research. Giroux (2007) posits that institutions of higher education can be foundational in these efforts as people "come together to talk, think critically, and act on their capacities for empathy, judgment, and social responsibility. Under such circumstances, the academy offers 'a hope that makes all hoping possible'" (p. 210). This last point is essential. Dialogue, which is a fundamental element of care, "cannot be carried on in a climate of hopelessness. If the dialoguers expect nothing to come of their efforts, their encounter will be empty and sterile, bureaucratic and tedious" (Freire, 2007, p. 92). If we rethink caring in the academy so that it is intertwined with hope for a more humane society, perhaps we may find a way out of the contradictions we encounter as carer-academics.

In the *JEC* article, I left my readers with a question: "How can we tilt the machine without *tilting* the machine?" Here, however, it seems more useful to rethink mechanistic metaphors because they do not provide leeway for envisioning what it means to develop humanistic care in the academy. In the song "Pinball Wizard" (Townshend, 1969), the band The Who tells the story of Tommy, "that deaf, dumb, and blind kid" who "sure plays a mean pinball." There is much we can learn from Tommy, who is not distracted by the buzzers and bells of the machine and beats the game by playing by its rules. Yet in caring, we are limited in what we can accomplish while we are trapped within the machine. Even while pushing against hegemonic boundaries, we still allow the game to continue. Acting otherwise is almost inconceivable because the hegemony of "what is" and "what has been" in education often feels so impermeable. Perhaps, to engage in a humanistic care, we must *tilt* the machine instead. This means thinking about education as tied to a greater political purpose, that is, education for a more humane humanity, which will never be accomplished on a pitched table.

—Tricia Kress

Affirmation, Incubation, and Metaphoric Connection: A Journey Through Your Books

Robert Lake

Dear Nel,

I am sitting in my office as I write this letter, at a desk that is almost completely covered by books that you have written or worked on in some way. I resonate with so much of your work that as I write my own contribution to this book, it is hard to know where to start or stop until I remember where I first read your work. It was your book *Philosophy of Education* (Noddings, 1998a), which I read when I was working on my master's degree in teaching English as a second language at the State University of New York, Albany. One of the concepts you discuss in this text is Buber's notion of confirmation as the "act of affirming and encouraging the best in others" (p. 192).This vibrant expression of care deserves much more attention than what could be covered in a letter, or a journal article. I think you should write a complete book on this.

At critical junctures in my experience, I have received words of affirmation that created a vision of possibility and direction that I might not have ever seen on my own. One of these experiences occurred during this same time period, when one of my professors encouraged me to continue my education in doctoral studies. Up until that moment, I had never given any serious thought to this idea. From that moment onward, however, the idea continued to grow on me, and a few years later I began a doctoral program in curriculum studies at Georgia Southern University. Now with my own students I look for ways to continually pass on this gift of helping them see the possibilities of personal breakthroughs as I get to know each student in a way that allows me to recognize aspects of development that are "struggling to emerge" (Noddings, 1998a, p. 192) but need encouragement and nurturing.

Early on in my doctoral program, I was introduced to your book *The Challenge to Care in Schools* (Noddings, 1992). By then I was so drawn in by your work, I decided to try to contact you personally. My talks with you were always short but very potent. I remember asking you a few questions while I worked on my dissertation. One of the questions I asked was "How do you maintain hopeful imagination in times like the ones we are living through now?" You said, "I work in my garden, hug my cat, and watch the sun rise over the ocean" (personal communication, September 4, 2006). I instantly understood and identified with this answer.

One thing I have learned about myself in the past 10 years especially is that I need to be outside almost every day, to feel fully alive. By this I am referring not only to the benefit of physical exercise but also the inspiration that can be gained by witnessing the way that nature continuously renews itself. We can draw from its forces by some variety of continual exposure to it. Your experience reminds me that in some ways, there is a connection between hope and the natural environment and the current system of schooling, in which test preparation has taken center stage; children are often deprived of experiences such as these.

The next book of yours that I pick up is *Awakening the Inner Eye: Intuition in Education* (Noddings & Shore, 1984). Since my doctoral research was on a curriculum of imagination, I find myself in concurrence with many of the ideas you present here. In fact, the cultivation of intuition in education is even more relevant today in this current climate of standardized and decontextualized subject matter derived from the canon of "official knowledge" (Apple, 1993). You are absolutely right about the need to instill in our students the capacity to "cultivate the Muse" (Noddings & Shore, 1984, p. 92) on their own. One of the ways you suggest that this is done is through an understanding of the value of incubation. I could not agree more. I suspect that in "incubation" personal metaphoric connections may be created that release personal understanding and empowerment that are the marks of valid learning experiences. Please allow me to briefly explain.

Almost everyone has had the experience of breaking through obstacles in problem solving after a short time of retreat and rumination on the nature of the difficulty. It may be anything from a plumbing problem, writer's block, or envisioning the theory of relativity, as in the case of Einstein. Obviously, some concepts need more applied contemplation than others, yet there are some characteristics of problem solving that are common to all humans and certainly should be considered and cultivated in the lives of those we teach.

But how might incubation be allowed to work in actual classroom practice? In order to answer that question, I will briefly share about the way metaphoric connections are created. Modell (2003) suggests that "what makes us uniquely human is an unconscious metaphoric process. Unconscious autobiographical memory, the memory of the self and its intentions, is constantly recontextualized, and the link between conscious experience and unconscious memory is provided by metaphor" (p. 25). Metaphor is not just a fanciful rhetorical device. Lakoff and Johnson (2003) posit that "metaphor is a neural phenomenon" (p. 256). Neural networks are created in the brain by the combination of subconscious memory and experience through metaphoric connections.

Consequently, metaphor is a tangible, physiological connector of the subconscious and conscious, the new and old, and the mental and physical through means of visual, verbal, somatic, and auditory concepts. Modell affirms this notion by further saying that "metaphor formation is intrinsically multimodal, as it must engage visual, auditory and kinesthetic inputs" (2003, p. 32). Curriculum must engage all these aspects in order for newly created personal connections to be formed. This holistic process needs incubation time. Sometimes this may occur while one is in a half state of sleep, or walking, or contemplatively reading, or just allowing students to have quiet time during the day.

One of the things I ask my preservice teacher candidates to observe in their field experience is the length of time a teacher allows before the "right" answer is spoken out. In today's frenzied pace of life where even "minute rice is cooked in a microwave" (Mike Shreve, personal communication, 1987), and "racing to the top" is the order of the day, teachers need to provide a nest of "affirmation" and "incubation" and wise restraint to enable each student to peck his or her own way out of the shell.

With love, much respect, and immense gratitude,

Robert Lake

Creating Pedagogies of Caring

Shaireen Rasheed

> We as teachers must engage our students in open, honest dialogue—sharing, guiding and staying with them as they struggle with problems we have not solved. (Noddings 2005d, p. 135)

At the beginning of every semester, my preservice students and I make an ethical commitment as part of our "pedagogic creed": to challenge dominant discourses of test-driven mandates, federal standards, and adherences to a standards-based curriculum. In the face of current glaring federal policies, the responsibility to "care" for a student's humanity becomes a daunting, almost impossible task. A task that you, Nel, as teacher, embodied in your interactions with your students; further, as an educator you created an ethical creed of "caring" to model our teaching pedagogies by.

It seems like a decade ago (and it was, given that it was 2000) at Columbia University, Teachers College when I started working on my dissertation with you as my dissertation chair. You not only encouraged me to further question the ethical goal of teaching but also modeled the ethics of caring in your interactions with all your students, including me. Through you I learned that an ethics of care requires that we take into account issues of difference when discussing notions of identity—even our own. Struggling to write a dissertation while being a new mother was a daunting task, but through your constant encouragement, you validated my identity as a woman and a mother, not just a doctoral student pursuing a tenure-track career in academia.

In your book *Caring: A Philosophical Approach to Feminine Ethics and Moral Education*, you say that ethical ideals have to do with caring and being cared for. Caring preserves both the group and the individual and limits our obligation so that it may be realistically met. It will not allow us to be distracted by visions of universal love, perfect justice, or a world unified under principle (Noddings, 2003a). Important ethical choices for you are not made according to rational principles. They depend on the will to be good, to remain in caring relation to the other.

A phenomenological pedagogy contextualized within your ethics of difference develops the historical and ontological basis for letting an "other" reveal to me that his or her world situation—different and conflictual—forms a locus from which to interpret reality. Being aware of this phenomenon on the part of educators is a central precondition of ethical recognition, namely, an ability not to treat as absolute any one perspective. Bringing teachers together in this context entails realizing that as educators we must talk across differences in a way that does not privilege one ideology over another. Your pedagogy of caring requires that teachers find new ethical conditions of possibility in order to unsettle powerfully entrenched and institutionalized notions of individualism.

Difference is something that all human subjects need to analyze and creatively engage with, instead of seeking to marginalize, deny, or obliterate it. Respect for the differences of the other is crucial in all exchanges. But through your research on caring I learned that it is important to move beyond that respect toward a new and more complex mode of living out the kind of identity that is understood only relationally through your ethics of care.

In your book *Stories Lives Tell*, you explain that collective thought and action require the continued critique of the exclusive reliance on separate knowing that has presented epistemic barriers to women and minority groups. What you propose instead are real democratic paradigms in which different individuals represent through dialogue a variety of voices that reflect their perspectives on social issues (Witherell & Noddings, 1991).

Within the context of curriculum, pedagogy of care becomes a process that takes into consideration social, political, and historical conditions, as well as the perspectives and considerations of the participants of that moment (Rasheed, 2006). And a caring, respectful dialogue then based on your ethics, Nel, among all those engaged in educational settings, serves as the crucible for our coming to understand ourselves, others, and the possibilities life holds for us. Caring then does not amount to grasping something in order to integrate it into our own world, but to opening one's own world to something or someone external and strange to it. Caring is a way of opening ourselves to the other and of welcoming this other, its truth and its world as different from ours.

To further elaborate the ethics of care we have to adopt Michel Foucault's distinction between morality associated with the history of different moral systems and institutions that enforce them and an ethics of care that refers to the work that self-transformative subjects perform on themselves in relation with others. How can these seemingly contradictory claims—the affirmation of becoming and the respect for the nonthematizable alterity of the other—be negotiated without evoking the Kantian reversibility of freedom and obligation (Ziarek, 2001)? The answer to this question lies in the theory that your ethics of care can be a condition of the ethical respect of the other because it negates any attempt to posit the particular universal into a universal norm.

Learning and, more important, thinking within this context become activities of the student's whole being. The task is to transform our selves at every moment in order to respect and care about the subsistence and becoming of both the other and myself as two radically different subjects. The journey for my students and me, as a result of implementing your ethics of care in our own pedagogies, is now more internal. The other is no longer the one whom I have to assimilate into my worldview, even though I know that this other is unattainable. On the contrary, the other is the one whom I must keep different from me. It is by maintaining the difference between our two subjectivities that I construct an ethics of relationality, that of mine and that of the other. And for emulating such an ethics in every aspect of your life, I am eternally grateful to you.

—Shaireen Rasheed

CHAPTER 3

Circles of Scholarship

Nel's academic work is well within the definition of what Emily Style says about the need for scholars to attend to "the scholarship of them-selves" to make textbooks of their lives, as well as scholarship on the shelves (cited in Wolf, 2001, p. 1). Women philosophers have led a needed revolt against decontextualized "ivory tower" approaches to educational thought and Nel Noddings has played a major role in this endeavor through a life as a situated philosopher. As the letters in this chapter clearly confirm, Nel's circles of scholarship begin with self reflection and then work outward to encircle families, communities, and nations.

A Tribute to an Idea

Eva Feder Kittay

Dear Nel,

One fine afternoon in Barcelona, as I was trying to catch up on some needed rest before the start of a workshop on care, I reencountered an idea that you first introduced in your landmark contribution *Caring*.

Despite the jetlag, my mind was racing with thoughts stimulated by a discussion over lunch with a few workshop participants. With laptop in tow, I sought out a local café and in a matter of an afternoon I had a new paper: "The Completion of Care." If the phrase sounds familiar, it is because it is your phrase. Over lunch we had debated the positive impact of care on the caregiver. In my writings I have often stressed the toll on the caregiver because I have wanted to avoid sentimentalizing what is often hard work and is underpaid or unpaid. But this emphasis on the burden of care creates its own distortion. We see dependency as merely negative, and the work of caring for dependents as "necessary work" (in the Marxian sense) best foisted on those who have little chance of doing more "fulfilling" work. You'll remember Simone de Beauvoir's devastating discussion of the tedium of work that can never be the occasion for transcendence. As feminists we need to reject this vision as well.

Nel, you know I am one philosopher who doesn't shy away from admitting the extent to which the concerns of my personal life stimulate much of my philosophizing. (I think we all do this, but for some, like myself, the spur is closer to the mind's surface.) I mention this, because while the care of my daughter Sesha, who with her profound dependency has initiated much of my thinking about care, I recently have also been dealing with the care of my 91-year-old mother. My mother, unlike my daughter, resists my care. She battles fiercely to maintain her independence, as she understands it. Rather than feel relief and gratitude that she is not "burdening" me, I feel sad, even angry, that she will not accept my care. (Apparently both the parent's resistance and the adult child's dismay are quite common.)

The lunchtime conversation helped me see that it was because I viewed caregiving as something that would enhance my well-being as well as hers that I was pained by this thwarted desire. And that's when it came to me—I recalled your words "Care must be completed in the other if it is to be a relation." My anger arose because my mother refused to complete my care, refused a certain sort of relation I wanted to have with her. (I also recalled that Joan Tronto speaks of the fourth or last phase of care as care that is recognized or received as care.)

Being in Barcelona, away from my books or a library, I wasn't then able to review what you said about this aspect of care. Yet the primary reason I needed to refresh my knowledge of this aspect of your work was because on first reading *Caring* I rejected the notion entirely. I think I was not alone, for with the exception of Tronto, who speaks of the reception of care as the final phase of care, I cannot recall anyone else who takes up the idea. (And I believe that Tronto never develops the notion). Until I could get back to my dog-eared copy, I would have to muddle through myself.

Why did I pay so little attention to this idea before? My thinking about dependency and care had its starting point in the care of my daughter Sesha. She, as you know, is totally dependent. This beautiful, sweet, delightful woman (she is now 40!) is unable to do anything for herself because of her serious cognitive impairments, her cerebral palsy, and her seizure disorder. I thought that to begin theorizing from the most extreme case would reveal features of care that more ordinary ones concealed. When we care for another, we may think, "I care for so and so now, and (implicitly) I expect that she will do the same when I need care," or, "As I make sacrifices for another, I expect her gratitude." I did not expect Sesha to reciprocate, nor did I expect expressions of gratitude. Her presence and well-being was all I sought. I required nothing from her. Thus, the idea that she needed to "complete my care" made little sense to me. If caring required some participation on my daughter's side, it wasn't clear that one could really say that one cared for her—and this was nonsense. So I outright rejected any idea that anything was required of the cared for.

Now that I also need to care for my mother, I finally get it. The contrasting experience makes me realize that Sesha has always completed my care, but has done so with a graciousness that has make it invisible. Had she shrieked and fought, and only at times cooperated, I would have understood this earlier. Because she is so lovely and loving, so cooperative, so responsive in her own quiet way, I was fooled into thinking that she was not an active participant in the care. (I think it is not unreasonable to consider this gracious taking up of care a moral virtue on her part. It is surely something that draws her caregivers close to her and something that they deeply appreciate about her.)

The more I thought about the completion of care, the richer the idea became. Just start with a simple thought experiment. I have a houseplant that needs watering. I see some clear liquid in a glass. Thinking it's water, I pour it into the pot. Unbeknownst to me, it was vinegar. Had I cared for the plant? Most would (and do) answer no. Thus, even from our ordinary understanding of care we can say, Nothing can count as caring if it is ineffectual or produces an ill effect for the being that is cared for.

Gilbert Ryle in his *The Concept of Mind* (2002) speaks of "achievement verbs" that are applicable only once the action is done. One only wins a race when it is won, not when it is run. The thought experiment shows that *care* is an achievement verb, which in turn means care is an act and must hit the mark if it is to be care. If this means that caring requires the cared for to "take up the action as care," then caring is also always relational. When I returned to your text, I found that many of my "discoveries" were already in *Caring*. You had already stressed that care requires action, not merely intention. In the expanded version of the paper, I make use of this point to reason that a care ethics can be neither a deontological nor a virtue ethics. Despite the resistance to the thought that an act can be morally worthy only when someone else responds, in *Caring*, you bite this bullet. I would add to your own excellent discussion a point that makes the stringency of this requirement more palatable. We can still say that a person who fails to care only because her caring is not taken up by the other is praiseworthy in altruism, heroism, or good-heartedness. But she cannot be morally praised as a carer.

I then lean on Bernard Williams's (1981) incisive discussion of moral luck to argue that an ethic of care is especially (though not exclusively) prone to the machinations of luck—luck respecting who we chose (or are assigned) to care for, the match of our skills to the task at hand, the possibility of forging a relationship, and so on.

While the emphasis on completion may look like it turns an ethic of care into a consequentialist ethic, that is a mistake. For all care, as you show so well, requires a motivational shift to the concerns and needs of the other. Benefiting the other without this intentional or attitudinal element no more yields care than does the attitude or intention alone. Consequently, from the consideration of completion of care, we arrive at the position that an ethic of care is sui generis.

Your contribution to the discussion of the completion of care is especially strong when you discuss it in terms of care's relationality. You say, "My caring has somehow to be completed in the other if the relation is to be described as caring" (Noddings, 1984, p.4). And you provide a wonderful phenomenological account of what a caring relationship looks like. I add a few points that may be of interest to you.

One is that if care needs to be completed in the other, then if there is no prior relationship, a relation must emerge or care will not happen. We must not, however, understand the emergent relationship as caregiving's intrinsic reward. The taking up of care is like the stage actor's having an audience that can witness and applaud the performance. It is the condition of the possibility of stage acting. But the actor (and carer) still needs to get paid.

The applause analogy is limited, however, because applause comes at the end of the acting. When caring is sustained, a deeper relationship can develop through the ongoing interaction of the carer and cared for. If one approach fails, the skillful caregiver shifts. A caregiver who normally moves quickly and efficiently may have to slow down to listen. The confident one may find herself needing to be more humble. (And now we return to the concerns I raised at the start of the letter.) In this dance where the caregiver leads and the cared for takes the cue, caregiving can become a source of self-shaping. The carer comes to discover internal resources and new vulnerabilities. The carer may uncover a need more pressing than the originating one, but also more strengths. Carer and cared for form a catalytic relationship in which neither's flourishing occurs in the absence of the other's flourishing. We have here a dialectical relationality that can sustain us through the long haul.

I end with a note of thanks and a tribute to an idea: the completion of care. It can be added to the many you have contributed, all of which have spurred the rapid development of an ethic whose insights transform our philosophy and our ethical life.

Warm regards,
Eva Feder Kittay

Caring and Moral Philosophy

Lawrence Blum

Dear Nel,

When I reflect on what your work has meant to me over the years, I inevitably come back to my encounter with *Caring*. My copy is of the original hardback. I no longer buy hardbacks because of the shrinking book space in my house and office. But the cover of that book, with the father looking tenderly at his infant pressed to his chest, and his wife or partner embracing both him and the child, is not something I was used to seeing in a philosophy book. It expresses the complex gender politics of your book but in some way counters your use of *feminine* in the book's subtitle: *A Feminine Approach to Ethics and Moral Education.* I know you have gotten a lot of grief for that subtitle over the years, that you had not at the time known of the feminist tradition in philosophy in which you would soon become one of the major figures, and that you are still somewhat ambivalent about whether that word might not express something important that you would not want the reader to lose sight of. I took the cover to emphasize that the ethic of care belonged as much to men as to women, and that even the tie between parent and young children, which is so often (and not wrongly) taken as fundamental to the female version of caring can be manifested in men if they would embrace it.

But the cover of your book was important for another reason that I am not entirely happy to admit, but perhaps this collection is a place in which I should do so. I'll have to place that reaction in context. I was at the time a moral philosopher, strongly trained in the Anglo-American tradition of the 1960s and 1970s. Utilitarianism and Kantianism were the reigning schools of thought. There was no defined alternative to them at the time. But I was never satisfied with these alternatives. A rare exception was stated by Bernard Williams when he pointed to some problems both views shared and had briefly suggested the importance of moral emotions in his 1965 paper. But hardly anyone was articulating an emotion-based alternative to the dominant rationalist schools of thought.

I had been fortunate to encounter Simone Weil's work in the late 1960s, when I was studying with Peter Winch. And I was especially enthralled with Iris Murdoch's 1970 collection of essays, *The Sovereignty of Good,* in which Weil's notion of "attention" was put to a creative ethical use. But no one was writing about either Weil or Murdoch, in the tradition with which I identified, and I did not really know how to do so myself. I couldn't figure out how to make the connections. You know, and knew at the time, that in 1980 I wrote a book on altruism; friendship; and altruistic emotions such as empathy, sympathy, and compassion, and I was pleased that you referred to it briefly in your book. But my work was still very tied to the Kantian paradigm as I was fighting my way out of it and against it.

I was familiar with the idea of "care," as I knew Carol Gilligan in the early 1980s and was in a philosophy/psychology study group with her. Nevertheless, your book was an absolute revelation. You developed the idea of caring so much further than Gilligan aspired to do. (As a moral psychologist, she had a different project.) Your book blew my mind, as we used to say in those days.

But, and here is the sort of embarrassing part, it felt like it was coming out of left field in relation to what I recognized as philosophical ethics. You just didn't have the same intellectual reference points. You talked about Buber! I just couldn't figure out where to place you in relation to what I knew.

But this is a minor point. I soon recognized the absolute originality of your book. I loved it. I have used it as a major text in every ethical theory course I have taught since then. You really helped me ultimately to find a way to bridge the divide between my "analytic" ethics background and the dissatisfactions I had with that tradition, and the Weil-Murdoch-Williams I had been drawn to.

I think the insights of *Caring: A Feminine Approach to Ethics and Moral Education* still have not been adequately taken up by mainstream moral philosophy. Feminist moral philosophy has certainly done a better job, and I was happy when your work started being discussed in *Hypatia* and elsewhere. But I still feel that there is more there that moral philosophy needs to learn from.

For me, a perfect example of this is the importance of caring relationships. As you have said in other subsequent writings, you are suspicious of turning caring into an individual virtue, and one main reason for this is that it omits the importance of caring relationships. I think that is absolutely right. Of course there has been much more philosophical attention to personal relationships since (and partly because of) *Caring*, and that is all to the good. Moral philosophers have not looked enough at the character of the good to the cared-for of being cared for. Normally someone who is cared for desires and appreciates the other's care, over and above the acts of help that this care leads to from the one-caring. I think this focus on ethics narrowly construed limits Michael Slote's important 2007 contribution to care ethics by leading him to neglect caring relationships (though he recognizes their importance).

My reading of *Caring* is that you were struggling to express what kind of good the good of a caring relationship is, in relation to the good of caring on the part of the one-caring and the good to the cared-for. Sometimes you say that unless the cared-for reciprocates or recognizes the caring, the one-caring cannot really be said to care. Other times you take the view that even if the one-caring can be spoken of as caring, without recognition, the relationship does not count as a caring relationship. I don't think you fully settle this not-merely-terminological dispute. But for me the larger substantive issue is that caring relationships embody a distinctive kind of goodness, and that goodness requires acknowledgment and response. You wonderfully describe the phenomenology of both parties to the caring relationship, capturing the rich complexity of this phenomenon. Here is an example of a passage that illustrates that richness for me: "The cared-for is free to be more fully himself in the caring relation. Indeed, this being himself, this willing and unselfconscious revealing of self, is his major contribution to the relation. This is his tribute to the one-caring, but it is not delivered up as tribute" (Noddings, 1984, p. 73). This kind of insight really helps us to understand the distinctive good of relationships. And I am not seeing the subtlety and richness of this kind of phenomenological insight in the moral philosophy literature with which I am familiar.

Thank you for your enriching the tradition of moral philosophy with which I identify, and also for your acts of professional kindness to me over the years.

–Lawrence Blum

The Toughness of Caring

Nicholas C. Burbules

Dear Nel,

I suppose I've reached a point in my life when I'm starting to recognize the many things I've learned from others. There aren't enough opportunities to say all the thank yous, or enough time. But this project provides me at least one opportunity, and a bit of time, to say thanks to you.

I'm sitting here with a copy of *Caring* alongside me, the first printing, the one with your name misspelled on the cover. I remember that I was lucky enough to be one of the first to read the manuscript, as a midprogram doctoral student, and you were kind enough to credit me in the acknowledgments (although I can't imagine I had anything of substance to contribute to the project).

I do know that this book was my first exposure to a kind of ethics that turned a lot of my ideas upside down, and which continues to shape my outlook to this day. While I didn't come to adopt an ethics of care, per se, I did come to appreciate the focus on personal character and relations with others that I now understand as part of a broader virtue ethics, the very old Greek notion that is having a renaissance lately. The idea that becoming an ethical person is a matter of self-conduct, and not rule following, was new to me. The idea that this self is always situated in a set of relations through which we learn, practice, and improve our exercise of these virtues makes ethics a central educational problem. The idea that emotion, judgment, and sensitivity to the particulars of a moral situation are key to the enactment of virtue still strikes me as a deep insight, and an invaluable corrective to the ways in which ethics are often discussed, even by many adherents of so-called character education.

All these understandings I trace to the first times I read this book. But it is hard for me to separate my appreciation of the book from the experience of knowing its author (and, really, why in a case like this should it be otherwise?). I can't read this book without hearing your voice saying the words and without thinking about the ways that you have lived what is written in it.

And this introduces the second theme I learned from the book, and from you. It touches upon a certain misreading, I think, of what an ethics of care requires of us. Too often your work is caricatured as a kind of "ethics of niceness." And perhaps the pink cover, the *Feminine Approach to Ethics* subtitle, and the legacy of certain residual stereotypes and essentialisms led readers to think that *caring* refers simply to a certain kind of sentimentalized maternalism.

You are, indeed, a very nice person. But the privilege of knowing you and seeing you in many situations remind me also of your capacity for anger, tough-mindedness, critique, and political outrage. The sentimentalized view would see these as deviations from caring, needing to be redeemed through compensatory tenderness. But that way of thinking reinscribes just the kinds of false dualities between caring and criticism, between tough- and tender-mindedness, between stereotypically feminine and masculine values that I see your work as challenging.

Returning to the book, I am reminded of my favorite (and often overlooked) section "The Toughness of Caring." I like these few pages because they challenge the easy position that caring is just a matter of niceness, that if we just care (and care more and more), that makes us a better person. Perhaps it is the experience of parenting, which I have now but didn't have when I first read the book, that makes me appreciate your observations that caring for others *requires* caring for the self. It is a dangerous thing (especially for women) to be told that giving and giving without regard for one's own needs is the way to be good, that altruism is a limitless moral injunction, that the needs of others are always more important than one's own. Many teachers, as my colleague Chris Higgins has written, are susceptible to these myths, often resulting in exhaustion and burnout. This goes for parents too.

I also like the passage "Our own ethicality is not entirely 'up to us'" (Noddings, 1992, p. 102), because it makes the relationality of our moral selves concrete and complicated. It is not in fact possible to always care, or to care for everyone (except in some attenuated and abstract sense). We love our children even when they are not always loveable; but sometimes part of that love is criticism, punishment, and allowing them to suffer the consequences of their bad decisions. We also fail, despite our desires, to be always the caring parents, partners, or friends with others we wish we could be. This is true not only because we are imperfect but because caring is not just one thing, but a complex set of feelings and judgments that entail things besides niceness, perpetual kindness, and giving. Of course sometimes caring (and caring for the self) involves saying no, or "I can't" or "I don't want to"–and with these choices always comes the possibility of going awry.

Then we come to that wonderful section on "my own ferocity" (pp. 100–101). This isn't just the ferocity of the mother lion protecting her cubs, but an acknowledgment of a human capacity that is constitutive of us as animals, which most of us never have occasion to act upon, but which is a part of us, tied to our capacity for anger and hate–which is to say tied to our capacity to care passionately and to act aggressively for what we think is right. Treating these qualities as somehow extramoral or as parts of ourselves we must always resist and keep in check is an oversimplification of our complex moral identity and agency. And that, too, is something I have learned from this book: If caring were a matter of just being nice to everyone, we would actually be disempowered as moral beings. Acknowledging that fact, and following it through to its consequences, yields a more interesting, a more complicated and difficult, ethic than I think many have taken from a cursory or secondhand reading of *Caring*.

Finally, it is this respect for what is interesting, complicated, and difficult in matters of ethics that I take most from your book, from our many conversations, and from watching the life you have lived. My own philosophical life and understanding are richer because of it. Thank you, Nel.

Nick

Nicholas C. Burbules

What Is Ethics . . . After "After All"?

Ann Diller

Dear Nel,

As I sit here gazing out at the spring greening of New Hampshire–apple blossoms opening, lilacs filling dooryards with their fragrance–I reflect on the flowering of your scholarship and find myself recalling a favorite passage from *Caring*: "It sounds all very nice, says my male colleague, but can you claim to be doing 'ethics'? After all, ethics is the study of justified action. . . . Ah, yes. But, after 'after all,' I am a woman, and I was not party to that definition. Shall we say then that I am talking about 'how to meet the other morally'? Is this part of ethics? Is ethics part of this?" (Noddings, 2003a, p. 95) I read it again and notice how I still feel an unmistakable thrill, a surge of excited energy. Why does this passage leap to mind in such a fresh way today?

I cannot remember a time when I was not already interested in ethics and concerned about moral education. But I can remember numerous times when I struggled over how best to teach ethics and moral education. Then came your book *Caring: A Feminine Approach to Ethics and Moral Education*. From my very first reading of *Caring*, I knew you had set forth a significant new "paradigm" with far-reaching consequences. And now, as I sit here reflecting back, I realize how transformative your work on the ethics of care has been in its influence on the way I teach teachers, on the teachers themselves, and on the course of my own scholarship. Your influence on my scholarship can, for the most part, be seen or inferred as a matter of published knowledge. In this letter, I want to tell you about a few highlights regarding your influence on the teachers themselves.

Shortly after the publication of *Caring*, I found myself presenting a synopsis of your book during a university summer session course for experienced teachers. What stands out vividly to this day was the eruption of enthusiasm from these teachers, particularly from the elementary school teachers, most of them women, a few men, all of whom "not party to" the standard definitions of *ethics* and of *moral education*. Their obvious delight arose from the recognition that finally someone had articulated what these teachers themselves felt to be their own deep sense of educational purpose. Someone had named, in print, what really mattered to them as teachers of young children. You not only acknowledged but also honored what they felt to be the guiding principles underlying their daily classroom interactions with students.

Thus began a recurrent phenomenon, one I have enjoyed witnessing over and over again: When teachers learn about your account of an ethics of care in education, which so clearly articulates their own felt sense of purpose as "one-caring," their sense of full-fledged membership in an ethical community is revived and strengthened. In recent years, this also includes something akin to membership in an "underground" ethical movement committed to sustaining relational values in a climate where genuine caring gets pushed aside, if not trampled or co-opted, in the press of frenzied "races" to reach the "top."

In addition, I've noticed that we, your readers, caregivers from various walks of life–teachers, other educators, parents, nurses, and so on–appreciate the precision of your scholarship, the phenomenological detailing that uncovers the complex relational labor entailed in caring. And at the same time, in conjunction with your illuminating excavation of the multifaceted nature of caring relations, you give central place to a crucial fact about the ethics of care, namely, that in any single moment a person can immediately gain access to and act upon this ethic. This crucial fact brings me to another point about your influence on teachers.

As you observe in your introduction to the second edition of *The Challenge to Care in Schools*, "People differ on what they mean by *caring*" (Noddings, 2005c, p. xiv). When I first taught an ethics of care to my preservice teacher education students, those preparing to teach in public high schools kept insisting there was "no way" they could "care for" what they envisioned as the 100 or more students attending their classes; they would "not have enough time!" Thus, I found myself pushing them to deepen their understanding of what constitutes the central focus of this ethic, namely, "how to meet the other morally": "When I care, I really hear, see, or feel what the other tries to convey. The engrossment or attention may last only a few moments and it may or may not be repeated in future encounters, but it is full and essential in any caring encounter" (Noddings, 2005c, p. 16).

Even such a brief chance meeting as one where "a stranger stops me to ask directions" can be an occasion for a caring encounter if "I listen attentively to his need, and I respond in a way that he receives and recognizes" (2005c, p. 16). Thus, as they studied and pondered your descriptions, my high school teachers came to realize that if we can pause in our personal trajectories, and temporarily bracket our own agendas, then the actual time required to "care" may take only a "few moments," during which we give a student our full complete attention. After all, in the last analysis, it is only in each present moment that we ever can, and do, "meet the other morally." Sometimes this may happen only once between a teacher and a particular student. In other instances, caring moments between teachers and students recur often enough to create and sustain caring relations; indeed, occasionally such relationships last for years, well after students have graduated.

In closing, I want to add a personal note. Although, in one sense, I "knew" from my first reading how your fierce unwavering focus on "meeting the other morally" aligns with your insistence on that transformative move away from the traditional preoccupation with justification, I now understand this more experientially. In another one of my favorite passages, you write, "As one-caring I am not seeking justification for my action; I am not standing alone before some tribunal. . . . I am not justified but somehow fulfilled and completed in my own life and in the lives of those I have thus influenced" (Noddings, 2003a, p. 95). In life, when we are experiencing moments of total "engrossment" during a caring encounter the question of "justification" simply does not arise. There is no time, no need, and no inclination, for adding on extraneous layers of preoccupation with "justified action." Our attention moves fully into meeting each other as ones-caring, and we do find ourselves "fulfilled and completed" . . . "after, 'after all.'"

–Ann Diller

The Seminar

David Flinders

Dear Nel,

This letter is to thank you for many years of mentoring. In the words allotted here I will focus on one particular gift, that of helping me understand the role of philosophy in curriculum studies. How I came to appreciate philosophy's contributions to my own field is a story that began in the early 1980s. I was a doctoral student, and together with my fellow students Steve Thornton and Lynda Stone, I ventured to the second-floor office of a new assistant professor (that would be you). Our purpose was to ask you to supervise an independent study on the writings of John Dewey. With the addition of several others the following semester, we formed a small seminar that met weekly at your home. Before I go on, however, I would like to juxtapose that seminar against my earlier (albeit very limited) study of philosophy.

As an undergraduate student, I was drawn to the "humanities" (literature, art, history, and the like), having concluded logically that the other disciplines (primarily math and science) were among the "inhumanities." In my first philosophy course we read David Hume, Kant, Russell, Sartre, and Kafka. The next semester I took a course, "Hesiod to Calvin," that surveyed earlier contributors to the canon. I was new to these "great thinkers" of Western civilization, and could not get enough of them. I remember cursing my high school teachers for keeping all this intellectual stuff a secret. In retrospect, my teachers were not entirely to blame for the milquetoast curriculum that was offered. I may not have been ready had my high school tried to introduce me to any type of ancient or modern philosophy. Worse, I might have fallen prey to the elitist tendencies of such a curriculum if poorly handled. Moreover, I would be hesitant to trade my comprehensive high school for anything that resembled an exclusive prep school. Many of my friends made it to graduation simply because they found a home in wood or auto shop, drama class, or band. From their experience and my own, I could see that nonacademic courses held their own value.

Nevertheless, the relevance of "eternal questions" for high school students remains an interesting curriculum question. Attending a school dominated by a single and exacting religion, learning something about Hume's skepticism might have made my life seem a little less insular. In this context, a discussion of freedom of thought may have sparked some interest as well. Subject to the military draft and listening each night to the news reports from Vietnam might also have served as fertile ground for discussing topics like duty, obligation, and obedience. Would I have been motivated to read Plato's *Republic* or the "Myth of the Metals?" More than 2,000 years after

Plato, the students in my high school were placed into three tracks that eerily paralleled bronze, silver, and gold.

Whatever opportunities may have been forgone early, my newfound interest in philosophy at the college level turned out to be all too fleeting. The reason for a change of heart was my third (and final) philosophy course as an undergraduate. The course was taught by a dour man whose solemnity for serious thinking was outpaced only by his contempt for other people. Philosophy was for philosophers. End of story. The Great Unwashed, undergraduates especially, were so far beneath this man as to be entirely irrelevant. People were nothing more than ants.

So I abandoned philosophy and turned to the more enjoyable craziness of trying to teach the English language arts to adolescents. Sometime later I landed in graduate school with Steve and Lynda knocking at your office door and begging for a Dewey seminar. At the seminar's first meeting I discovered something odd. The others whom you had invited to join our original group were not other graduate students but rather Stanford faculty. We ended up with six or seven professors and three students. Each week we read and discussed one of Dewey's books, but outnumbered two to one, my student peers and I could hardly get a word in edgewise. I remember listening a lot, and what I listened to was the respectful and passionate dialogue about ideas. It was an apprenticeship of thinking carefully and rigorously about the intellectual traditions of education.

The professors in the seminar represented Stanford's curriculum studies program faculty, and as such their backgrounds and areas of expertise cut across a wide range of subject areas, ideological positions, and research specializations. Beyond yourself, Nel, only one other person in the group could be considered a philosopher of education. Nevertheless, each person around the table knew Dewey well and readily linked his ideas to his or her area of expertise. Dewey was common ground, and the seminar was inclusive in this sense of sharing mutual respect. It was not long before my early undergraduate excitement for thinking about "big ideas" was reawakened.

I learned something about Dewey's philosophy in our seminar, which may have been no small accomplishment in my case. But much more was gained in the way of what Dewey called "concomitant" learning. These unanticipated lessons included how to question one's own assumptions and the assumptions of others respectfully as well as how to decide what is worth disagreeing about. I also learned the importance of an idea's history and the recurrence of educational values over time. I learned that some contradictions we must learn to live with unresolved. I did not actually learn all these important norms of scholarship in a single semester, but our Dewey seminar was a good beginning. It was also symbolic of the type of intellectual apprenticeship that includes, when extended over time, core values as well as tricks of the trade. Philosophers and other academics know that critical analysis alone will not end poverty, global strife, or institutional bigotry. Lamenting such limitations may be good for our humility, but it still misses the point that critical thinking remains the bread and butter of education. And education, in turn, remains one of our most enduring forms of social change.

                                                                    —Dave Flinders

---

What It Means to Be a Public Intellectual

Kathleen Kesson

Dear Nel,

When I was a new graduate student, and dared to think I might become a philosopher of education, I read all the Great Dead White Men. I reveled in their lofty ideas and fancied myself a writer of Great Books too, a member of that elite club of thinkers. Alas, reality intervened. A single mother of four young boys, I found that my pragmatically informed career choices led me to teacher education, rather than a department of philosophy. Although I wrote and published enough to successfully rise on the academic career ladder, I consistently disappointed myself in terms of measuring up to our philosophical forefathers. I consoled myself, however, with the excuse that these Great Thinkers had probably always had others (women) to do their domestic labor for them, someone else to cook and clean and raise the kids while they smoked pipes and gazed out their windows or walked in the meadows pondering the Big Questions. They certainly weren't cooking for four young boys; chauffeuring them to soccer, baseball, and music lessons; working multiple jobs to support a family, et cetera. This reasoning worked pretty well for me, providing me with the exemption I needed for my shortcomings . . . until I came across Nel Noddings, philosopher par excellence, *and* mother of ten. Ten! How in the world did you do it, Nel?

Your ability to live a full life that encompassed both the domestic and the professional did more than just spark feelings of inadequacy, however. You provided an important model for the integration of these spheres into a larger whole. Your interest in, and commitment to, more "conventional" feminine interests—home, family, care—was a challenge to prevailing ideological frames that dismissed the interest in caring for children and other domesticities as an inferior pursuit. You were, in that sense, a harbinger of newer versions of feminism in which women are demanding acknowledgment of and support for a broader range of life pursuits and purposes.

When asked to contribute to this collection, I wondered which of your many valuable contributions to focus on. So much of your work has spoken to me—your treatises on intuition, caring, justice, moral education, feminism, and imagination—the list of topics to which you have applied your immense intelligence seems endless. The issues close to your heart echo the reasons I chose to enter the field of education. You consistently ask the important questions: What is worth knowing? What should we teach? How should we treat each other? How can we create a better world?

I chose to focus on your wonderful book, first presented as a John Dewey lecture in 1991, *Educating for Intelligent Belief or Unbelief* (Noddings, 1993). I appreciate this book, in part, because you wrestle with themes that I too have engaged with over the years. But more important, it is written in a way that embodies the integration of several qualities that exemplify the kind of intellectual work that I have come to value even more than that of the Great Thinkers whom I once emulated.

Compassion. Although I know from watching you in action that you do not suffer fools gladly, in this piece you demonstrate a remarkable tolerance for foolish ideas. And this is because at the heart of the book is an inquiry into the nature of truth. While you gently urge readers to "appreciate the power" of even messages that are irrational or superstitious, you also urge them to "examine the logic." Without negating the impulses and desires toward religious experience that many people hold, and without attempting to debunk these, you are carefully insistent that all ideas should be subject to scrutiny and skepticism, especially if they are to be brought into the arena of the public school. This is a welcome contrast to the extremes of both positions: the inflexible and intolerant ravings of fervid fundamentalists *and* the derisive mocking of such debunkers as Bill Maher, as in his film, *Religulous*. Neither Maher nor the fundamentalists are likely to provoke true believers, be they religionists or atheists, into examining their beliefs; you are, because you treat all beliefs with respect, calling on "our good conscience" in engaging people of wildly diverse perspectives in discussions of religion. You seem aligned with Dewey here, both in his appreciation for the longings of the human spirit to reach beyond ourselves and to transcend the ordinary, and in his commitment to collaborative inquiry as the ultimate road to truth.

Courage. It takes intellectual courage in the current highly charged, ideologically driven times, to speak the unspeakable and propose the unpopular: that the story of Adam and Eve should be examined along with other creation "myths" in our literature classes, that witchcraft and goddess worship are as deserving of our critical attention and appreciation as are the Big Three Monotheisms, that we should examine the Janus face of religion—both its impulses toward love and brotherhood and its historical evils and abuses. That the "public" finds it so difficult to engage in a reasoned examination of religious beliefs suggests that we have a ways to go before your proposals meet enthusiastic responses from school boards, but kudos to you for putting such dangerous ideas forth!

Integrity. In this book you speak of the importance of pedagogical neutrality, the need for teachers to clearly present as many sides of these questions as possible so as to engender the deepest thinking of our students. In this sense, the medium really is the message, for the book is an exemplar of pedagogical neutrality. As I finished this latest reading, I found myself wondering, Is Nel a Catholic? a Wiccan? a Unitarian? an atheist? How superb, to have written almost 150 pages on belief, and not made your own obvious! This is an intellectual ethic that we can all but hope to aspire to.

Clarity. Oh, what a blessing to write in language that is clear and comprehensible. While Hegel, Heidegger, and the other Great Thinkers (including most contemporary philosophers) may never be read by anyone save graduate students in philosophy, your work is destined to be read by everyday folks: teachers, parents, interested community members. You have, in this way, rescued philosophy from a fate in which it is only read by other philosophers, far removed from the concerns of everyday life and inaccessible to most people. Not once in these pages do you talk down to your audience. Instead, you have mastered the art of communicating complex ideas in ways that most educated readers can easily understand and engage with. I think this makes you a genuine "public intellectual," and I'm quite sure Dewey would approve.

Sincerely,

Kathleen Kesson

The Heart's Truth: Seeing Philosophy Anew Through the Lens of Care, and Care Anew Through the Lens of Philosophy

Bruce Novak

Dear Nel,

Since early adolescence I have seen myself as a "philosopher." But I don't think I'm alone, particularly among philosophers of education, in saying that what I understood it *meant* to be a philosopher underwent a major transformation and became both deeper and clearer through knowing you and your work. What greater debt can one have than to someone who helps you entirely rearticulate the meaning of your life's calling?

As a way to begin to repay that debt, and perhaps to add some interest to it, I will share a number of thoughts I've had over the years—some inspired directly by you and your work, some coming to me as corollaries and further developments—about what the "love of wisdom" looks like when "care" is seen as integral to it, and also about what caring words and action look like when they are seen cumulatively as working within an inherited world of "loving wisdom."

Pascal famously said, "The heart has its reasons that reason knows not of." For me—and for many others, I'm sure—the greatest gift of your thinking has been to coherently open educational and public discourse to the "heart's reasons," the heart's truth, in ways that have already borne much fruit and that I think have the potential to bear even more in coming years. Here, then, are a few words I hope might be of some help in the ripening process.

Philosophy as Solicitude: Care and the Philosophical Tradition

I first met you in person when, with a call from my friend and your student Betsy Burris, you were the keynote speaker for my first academic conference, "Fostering Transformations in Teachers and Learners," for the Assembly for Expanded Perspectives on Learning of the National Council of Teachers of English, in the summer of 1998 in the mountains of Colorado. This was not a group of philosophers, and you didn't speak to them in explicitly philosophical terms. Down the road, though, I came to see that the main talk you gave—"'Caring About' Is Not Enough"—was in deep dialogue with important works from the philosophical tradition, in ways that not long after helped me rearticulate the meaning of that tradition.

It focused on a distinction between "caring about" the affairs of the world, with which most of education is occupied, and "caring *for*" others as fellow beings, which should be, but is not, the central concern of education as it is currently practiced, especially within the educational systems of large industrial nations. I didn't realize until I got back to my graduate school classes that fall, which coincidentally included a two-semester seminar in Heidegger's *Being and Time* (1962) with the philosopher Jonathan Lear, that this talk had clearly knowingly adapted for everyday pedagogical use two of Heidegger's central terms: *Umsorge*, "caring about," interest, pure and simple, and *Fürsorge*, "caring for," solicitude for another being *as* another being. In "caring for," as you put it in *Caring*, my ordinary interest is "displaced"; "my *I* becomes a *duality*," entering the realm of life Martin Buber calls the "I-Thou" relationship.

When I spoke to you about this a few years later, you told me you'd "never warmed to Heidegger." As someone who *had* warmed to him, though, I began to look at the whole text of this work—more than any other, acclaimed as the most important philosophical work of the 20th century—as revolving around the understanding and generation of "caring for": what it means for education, for history, for politics, and through all these, for philosophy itself. I found, for instance, this statement toward the end of the book: "Practical . . . pedagogy, in the broadest and deepest sense . . . is the soul of all true philosophy and the truth of Plato and Aristotle" (Heidegger, 1962, p. 454).

This led me back to Plato and Aristotle. You and other feminists have written about these two as repressing the feminine aspects of thought and moral life, and many postmodernists have written about them as the originators of "phallocentric" metaphysics. What I found, though, was that it was still possible to read them otherwise, depending on what parts of their writings are highlighted. Here, for instance, is Plato, in his Tenth Letter, defining *true* philosophy *as* solicitude, and *not* as either metaphysical or logical argument: "Dedication, trustworthiness, and sincerity—that, say I, is the genuine philosophy. Other kinds of wisdom and cleverness that lead to other results I believe I name correctly when I term them mere embellishments and parlor-tricks" (Plato, Epistle X, 1925).

Aristotle never says things this clearly—and explicitly vaunts contemplation, not solicitude, as the highest virtue. But his *second* highest virtue, and the one he spends by far the most time talking about—two full books of the *Nichomachean Ethics*—is "friend-ship." And his conception of true friendship, and with it true politics, is not far from Plato's understanding of true *philosophy*: the dedicated pursuit of "like-mindedness" through an ethos of magnanimity, reliability, and sincere solicitude. Aristotle divides "intellectual virtue" or "wisdom" into two parts—theoretical and practical—that is still an active part of our intellectual heritage. But he could as well have added a third, and perhaps most important, part, called "solicitous" or "integrative" wisdom, *both* practical and theoretical as it seeks to bring separate natures into harmonious coexistence. As "I become a duality" when I am able to care, solicitous wisdom seeks to make sincere friends out of those whose interests may seem indifferent or inimical to one another.

"Care" cannot be said to *permeate* the Western philosophical tradition. Concern with it is conspicuously absent from the British empiricists—Bacon, Hobbes, and Locke—whose thought was most influential in the political founding of the United States. But there is certainly, lying within that tradition, a significant *sub*tradition of thinking about care, starting with Plato and Aristotle, proceeding through Augustine, continuing through Rousseau and Kant, and blossoming, to my mind, in Heidegger, his friend Karl Jaspers, and their mutual student Hannah Arendt—as well as in your own work. And it, of course, is up to the future to decide what the *central* tradition and the *central* values of "the love of wisdom" should be.

Solicitude as Philosophy: "Loving Wisdom" in Everyday Life

Philosophy has often been pronounced as dead in this supposedly "postmodern" age. But that may just be because so many "moderns" simply entirely misconstrued what philosophy was. Your helping us see the care at the heart of philosophy thus also helped us bring philosophy back to life—or rather, to see that it was only dead if we failed to give our hearts to it.

There is another side to this awakening, or reawakening, though. It has to do with seeing "the love of wisdom" in places it has not traditionally been seen—that wherever sincere solicitude is found, there too is the love of wisdom. What the philosophically trained physician Rachel Remen calls "kitchen table wisdom"—finding meaning, and healing, through becoming immersed in one another's stories—may actually count more as authentic philosophy than many a logical treatise, which in Plato's terms may be nothing more than a collection of sophisticated manipulative "parlor tricks."

I, in fact, took the title for this offering, "the heart's truth," from the title of a book I found at a philosophy conference about what happens at the core of the profession of nursing. When I began my career as a teacher, I saw that I didn't know a lot about the practice of care, and sought extensive mentoring in it—which, more than any intellectual training I ever received, was central to whatever real success I have seen in this calling. And when I began to teach prospective teachers about what the heart of teaching was about, I found that, almost without exception, each person who chose to enter the profession had an influential teacher whose caring personhood was absolutely central to his or her decision. What keeps us from seeing "dedication, trustworthiness, and sincerity," wherever they occur, as philosophy in deep action in the world?

Sister Joan Chittister, in *Job's Daughters: Women and Power* (1990), distinguishes "nurturant" and "integrative" forms of power, which add to life, from "exploitative," "competitive," and "manipulative" forms of power as it is traditionally conceived, as a zero-sum game in which there are always only winners and losers. Our current political structures require the life-enhancing forms of power to work mostly in the shadows. What, though, if we were to envision and enact alternative structures—the "partnership" structures envisioned by our mutual friend Riane Eisler?

We are now experiencing times in which what has been called "civilization" is clearly approaching ruination, and in large part through our enfranchising life-sucking forms of power over life-enhancing ones. What, though, if, in the words of the poet Browning (1902), we could come collectively to see

> . . . the worth of love in [our] estate,
> And what proportion love should hold with power

In [our] right constitution; love preceding
Power, and with much power, always much more love. (p. 71)

Philosophy, thanks to you and others through long stretches of human time, may just be, as Toni Morrison has said of history, "about to take its first unfettered breath" (2008, p. 186)! And this is something many of those who have never begun to think of themselves as "philosophers" may come to be deeply grateful for.

Yours,

Bruce

Manifesting More Than Can Be Said

Molly Quinn

The world is upside-down, and is suffering so much, because there is so very little love. . . . We have no time for our children, . . . for each other; . . . to enjoy each other. . . . People who love each other fully and truly—they are the happiest people in the world. (Mother Teresa, 2007, p. 92).

> Teach your children to love one another.
> Teach your children to have respect for each other.
> Teach your children to share.
> Teach your children, because nowadays, many schools do not teach
>   these things . . .
> All over the world there is terrible suffering, terrible hunger for love.
>   (pp. 96, 97)

Love is not something that fossilizes, but something that lives. . . . And where does this love begin?—right in our hearts. We must know that we have been created . . . not just to be a number in the world, not just to go for diplomas and degrees, this work and that work. We have been created . . . to love and to be loved. (p. 89)

Dear Nel,

Recently—issuing from my efforts to theorize justice, and justly theorize, in curriculum studies, I have been led to the study of world leaders, like Mother Teresa, as visionary teachers of justice and peace. Of course, with her, others—Gandhi, King, the Dalai Lama—all emphasize the cultivation and challenge of love, and compassion, and action that affirms life and peace. Particularly, though, as I read Mother Teresa, I was again reminded of your work. For as she, as she lived, tirelessly beckoned all to her "revolution of love," so too have you persistently called for a revolution of care in the upside-down world of schooling, drawing our attention ever to the import of, and summoning us continually to, an education of the heart as much as the mind (and body). By this, I have been much influenced and greatly inspired, and for this, I am most and ever grateful.

A subsequent reading of Mary Poplin (1999) on lessons from Mother Teresa for the global classroom in a new century confirmed my thought of affiliation. Poplin highlights what she has found in her work to be the issue most often raised in schools—that of relationships, and questions our negligence in even acknowledging, much less addressing, the genuine challenge of cultivating nourishing relationships. She describes only briefly the care of Mother Teresa, with whom she once worked: strong and sacrificial, grounded in a deep respect that sees the divine in every person encountered, such that the manner in which every task and every person attended to is a sacred one— a care embodying a profound reverence for life itself. Then, she refers her audience to "the real expert on caring in education, Nel Noddings" (p. 31).

While some of my first philosophical interests in care emerged from Heidegger's (1962) analysis of the very meaning of human "being" as care in its temporality, particularly with respect to its constitutionally "being-towards-death," presently I find myself drawn to Arendt (1993), and the care that is grounded in what she calls the essence of education, "natality, the fact that human beings are *born* into the world" (p. 174). Herein is attentiveness to being-toward-life as well, and being-for-love, of course also integrally and inextricably tied to the fact of human mortality. Herein, too, I have returned to your work, realizing just how radical it is—ever excavating and elucidating love as at the root of life well lived, and thus of an education well borne—and come to glean insight and inspiration from it anew.

For you so cogently remind us that even "a moment taken from philosophical analysis to water a plant affirms life *manifests something more than can be said*" (Noddings, 1993, p. 14; emphasis added). Although an educator with much of import to say, although a philosopher endowed much with a talent for sharp and keen analysis, you draw from this acute example of Wittgenstein to illustrate how that which is most important eludes academic knowledge and scientific inquiry—you endorse care respecting the unsayable affirmation of life, and a "life-oriented education" embracing such care, in which too "all questions are sacred" (p. 14). In critically highlighting another example in which the death of a child is suggested by another scholar to have at one time *not* been "nearly unbearable," you do such in recognizing and challenging a fossilizing, "callous death orientation" by which conventional education is so powerfully constituted (p. 12).

You commend an education that awakens us to our own existence, to questions that matter to us concerning it, embedded in "the love that precedes and accompanies birth, the parental love that nurtures and sustains,

. . . this love that literally and metaphorically says 'yes' to life . . . as a promise of goodness and openness . . . . enhanc[ing] moral communion" (p. 13). Such does call to mind mother love, yet in seeking the creation of contexts wherein care itself can thrive, and via outcomes commensurate with justice, you complicate our gendered constructions of care and challenge us all to adopt this posture.

In thinking of you, in fact, a flourishing context of communion most fittingly comes to mind: I recall the great pleasure of time spent in your presence, and together in conversation, some years back in the intimate setting Louisiana State University's Curriculum Camp afforded. There, in Robert, Louisiana, in the woods at a small retreat center—over a fireside chat, a cup of coffee, a glass of bourbon, a sampling of Creole cuisine; amid Cajun dancing, keynote presentation, academic dialogue, airport transport—much of what I read in your work came to life for me through this direct engagement with you personally . . . in relationship. I remember the simple wisdom you expressed regarding the error of telling children to "always do your best" as though all things mattered equally, as though discernment did not matter in the art of living, and learning—which raised my consciousness, too, about my own teaching and orientation to living. I remember your generous counsel and genuine care respecting my work at the university and the journey to both sanity and success therein. And I shall never forget the memorable drive with you and your husband to the airport, where I came to know something more of your own journey, both personally and professionally—mostly through your husband's delightful stories.

Only now as I reflect, too, on the breadth and depth of your work—on intuition, belief, intelligence, caring, justice, happiness—do I realize how rather imitative has my own story here been of yours—studying imagination, faith, ignorance, hospitality, justice, peace, and love; how profoundly indebted I am to you and to your thought, for which specifically I seek here to offer deepest admiration and thanks.

Yours affectionately,

Molly Quinn

Ethical Caring in Cultural Context

Sabrina Ross

Caring involves stepping out of one's own personal frame of reference into the others. When we care, we consider the other's point of view, his objective needs, and what he expects of us. Our attention, our mental engrossment is on the cared-for, not on ourselves. (Noddings, 2003a, p. 24)

Dear Nel,

Although we have never met personally, your writings on caring and moral education have greatly influenced both my thinking and my classroom teaching practices. As a teacher educator, I am charged with helping future teachers gain an appreciation for the various forms of cultural diversity they will encounter in our increasingly diverse public schools. Your work highlights the broader social implications of caring in education and has taught me that my classroom interactions with preservice teachers can affect their future interactions with their students.

I take seriously your argument that ethical caring—caring not because I want to, but because I believe it is the right thing to do—allows those who are cared for to develop ideal images of themselves. My hope is that the students I interact with will realize ideal images of themselves as educators who are thoughtful of the diverse frames of reference and varying needs of the students they will teach; in short, I hope they will be educators who engage their students in acts of ethical caring.

Caring: A Feminine Approach to Ethics and Moral Education enabled me to perceive my classroom practices as moral acts that, although regarded as "odd" and inferior when compared with male-centered approaches to morality (Noddings, 2003a, p. 3), can contribute to the greater good in both education and the wider social environment. This letter serves as a form of thanks to you for your scholarship and its influence on my teaching and scholarship.

I first encountered *Caring* in a doctoral course on the moral dimensions of education. Your book, along with Carol Gilligan's *In A Different Voice* (1982), highlighted the vast differences between male-centered and female-centered approaches to morality and the ways in which women's approaches to moral action through relationships of connection and care are socially undervalued (Gilligan, 1982; Noddings, 2003a). Using examples of parents and teachers as models of ethical caring, your book demonstrated ways in which intentional connections between public and private spheres could facilitate my own efforts at ethical caring in the classroom.

Honoring these connections has forced me to negotiate the tensions my own lived realities bring to my practices of ethical caring. Recognizing the influence of very different lived realities on men's and women's moral reasoning, you wrote, "men intellectualize, abstract, and institutionalize that which women treat directly and concretely" (Noddings, 2003a, p. 130). There is a marked difference between the abstract, distanced reasoning generally associated with male-centered ways of being and the reasoning made through personal connections to real events commonly associated with feminine ways of being; these different lived experiences result in women's particular approach to moral reasoning as an ethic of care (Noddings, 2003a).

It was your emphasis on the differences in lived experiences between men and women and the resulting differences in men's and women's approaches to morality that encouraged me to more deeply explore how differences in my own lived experiences, as an African American woman, might influence my approach to ethical caring. While caring at its best promises reciprocity when the cared-for answers the acts of caring with "recognition and spontaneous response" (Noddings, 2003a, p. 78), caring necessarily involves aspects of self-sacrifice by focusing attention "on the cared-for, not on ourselves" (p. 24).

Historically, African American women in the United States have been forced through social and economic pressures to engage in acts of self-sacrifice, serving as nurturers and caretakers of others on slave plantations and later as domestic service workers; while the historical factors that limited the life options of African American women to caretaking roles have been altered, sociocultural perceptions of African American women as natural caretakers continue to influence African American women's social interactions and role expectations (Collins, 2000; Giddings, 1984). In my attempts to implement aspects of ethical caring in my own teaching, I have worried about ways in which my acts of self-sacrifice within the classroom could reinscribe socially enforced controlling images of African American women as self-sacrificing nurturers whose care for others must necessarily take precedence over their own needs (Collins, 2000).

In their book *Race-ing Moral Formation. African American Perspectives on Care and Justice*, Vanessa Siddle Walker and John Snarey (2004) highlight ways in which the lived experiences of African Americans has resulted in unique moral dilemmas in, among other things, the emphasis placed on self-care and the care of others. As an African American woman, my negotiation of tensions between ethically caring for my students and practicing self-care reflects the moral dilemmas highlighted in Walker and Snarey's book. My moral negotiation of these tensions is played out in complicated ways each day that I enter the classroom and has necessitated my use of an ethic of care reflective of my general lived experiences as a woman and my particular lived experiences as an African American woman (Roseboro & Ross, 2009).

What is significant here is not that the frame of reference I employ in modeling an ethic of care differs somewhat from the one you outlined in *Caring*. What is significant is that *Caring* brought to my attention the ways that women's lived experiences encouraged approaches to moral education that were equally important to those encouraged by men's lived experiences. By highlighting relationships between women's caring and moral education, you showed me the importance of engaged and caring relationships for human betterment. Just as important, you created a space within which I could explore the implications of your work within the cultural context of my own teaching and scholarship. For these things, I thank you.

−Sabrina Ross

On a Brain Catching Fire

Barbara Stengel

Dear Nel,

I don't remember when I met you. It probably happened in passing at a professional conference in the early 1980s. I didn't notice the "fire" at first. That came later. I do know that I invited you to Millersville University in 1991 to give the Anna Funk Lockey Lecture in Education. The fire was burning brightly by then, but I had no idea how long and how intensely it would be ablaze.

When you came to give the Lockey Lecture, I noticed that you don't waste many words; words fuel thoughts and I think you save them for your writing. It's one of the things about you that inspire me: you are a scholar who writes *every day*. And every day you bring a woman's active intelligence to bear on education and the issues emanating from this work.

I think it was while reading your early work on caring that I first understood how frequently smart scholars misunderstand what other smart scholars are trying to say. So many readers, both supporters and critics, missed your painstaking phenomenological analysis of caring, and missed too the implication that caring was a verb and not, or at least not merely, a feeling. Despite that, you always seemed to understand that being taken seriously, even if misunderstood, is a great compliment, and always an opportunity for dialogue and engagement.

Through dialogue and engagement in person and in writing, you demonstrated that *caring* is a verb and *happiness* is not a dirty word—and you offered the fruits of your philosophical labor in so many venues and versions over the past 3½ decades. An observation that seems to be elegant philosophy from one angle turns out to be best pedagogical practice from another angle and caring common sense from yet another.

In each of your books, I encountered insight both impressive and useful. Your painstaking analysis in *Women and Evil* (1989) remains underappreciated. That evil can be understood as unnecessary pain, unnecessary separation, or unnecessary helplessness is so clearly accurate, so blessedly concrete, and so promising a guide for moral judgment and ethical action. Your analysis has become a kind of mantra guiding students in the principal's certification program at my university. Years after they complete the program, they come back telling stories of how that analysis has helped them over and over again to make tough decisions as school leaders.

Your John Dewey Lecture turned monograph, *Educating for Intelligent Belief or Unbelief* (1993), is an unparalleled guide for treating religion—in our schools and in our interpersonal lives—intelligently but not insensitively. I

wish it were required reading for school board members and science and social studies teachers! I've kept your words in mind as I have taught intelligent
fundamentalist students and unintelligent atheists in this state system university set firmly in a location that brings creationists and evolutionists into close
and sometimes uncomfortable proximity. Your work is a constant reminder
that developing what Dewey would call "the method of intelligence" is perhaps the surest way to navigate the shoals associated with diverse religious
commitments.

Only a parent would take happiness seriously as an educational goal as
you do in *Happiness and Education* (2003b). And only a parent of more than
one child recognizes as clearly as you do that each individual's happiness
must be forged and understood in the process of living and not simply found
and acknowledged in a moment of discovery. And only a parent who has
watched those multiple children fall down and get up again taller than before
knows deep in her sometimes pain-laden heart that happiness and unhappiness are both implicated in the natural, intellectual, emotional, spiritual, and
interpersonal growth of each human person. A parent's perspective helps the
educator (at least *this* educator) to make sense of two conflicting intuitions:
that happiness is somehow better than unhappiness both in the classroom
and outside it and that some unhappiness in the course of growing up—
growing smart and growing good—is not only unavoidable but may be absolutely necessary.

When I consider how you and your work have affected me and my work,
I think not only of this range of ideas but also of a particular moment in time.
You were responding to a panel of presentations titled "The Impact of the
Moral on Teacher Education" at the AERA meeting in Montreal. The date
was Friday, April 23, 1999, the 3rd day after the shootings at Columbine High
School. In the 72 hours between the shootings and the session, I had heard no
one else mention these events from a podium. While there were many who
spoke of it in the conference hallways, the program went on as though the
world of education and schooling had not been altered significantly—until you
stood up. You noted that you couldn't talk about the moral dimensions of education without acknowledging this event that called into question everything
we had taken for granted about schools and safety and the moral expectations
that framed our work as educators. You were right.

You always said that if you want to know what matters to you, look at
what you do. The moral awareness, responsiveness, and responsibility that
you wrote about throughout your career were on display that day.

Nel, you were nearing 50 years old when you *began* your career at Stanford. As many scholars were sputtering out you were just getting fired up.
Speaking of getting fired up, have you read Christiane Northrup's *The Wisdom
of Menopause*? I thought of you when I read it. Northrup says that the brain

catches fire at menopause, that women's minds (specifically, the temporal lobe and the limbic system) are hormonally rewired in the days, months, and years before the menses pause. As she puts it, perimenopause is the mother of all wake-up calls. Women who have been hormonally lulled into the docility required to remain with children even when they mouth off, stay up late, and eat you out of house and home shift into a definitely not docile period of creativity and, dare I say, wisdom.

I think your brain caught fire, Nel. I'm glad it did, and I'm not the only one. Legions of philosophers—feminist and not—know the power of your relentless intelligence. Legions of educators know the pedagogical value of your insight. But some of us know more. Some of us know that caring and intelligence and happiness are, for you, not simply phenomena to be analyzed, but practices to be lived. It has been my privilege to live these with you, if only in a small way.

With deep affection and even greater respect,

Barb Stengel

Caring in Practice

Dilafruz Williams

Dear Nel,

I vividly remember my reaction to Karl Hostetler when he contacted me in 1996 with an outline of his proposed book *Ethical Judgment in Teaching* (1997), stating that he had "paired" philosophers of education to respond to seven hypothetical ethical cases in his book and wanted me to participate. The reaction was one of anxiety, since he had paired me with you to respond individually to a case ("Self and Others") and then we had to comment on each other's responses.

I was nervous; you were a well-established and known scholar whose writings also informed my own. I had used your books and articles on caring in my classes. I was nervous given your stature in the field. I was nervous particularly about the proposed "rejoinder" with a senior philosopher such as you. I expressed my hesitance to Karl, who talked me out of the excuses and into considering the project. He rightly pointed out that your life's work, after all, was about "care" and that he knew you as someone who was not arrogant—but rather, thoughtful and humble, even when demanding high standards of everyone. Instead of the "case study," he and I spent more time talking about you—a teacher, a scholar, a mentor, to so many of us. Most important, as we talked, I remembered your decency. In every encounter with you over the years—whether at Philosophy of Education or American

Educational Research Association conferences (especially, with our interests in the John Dewey Society)—what has stood out for me is your genuine interest in listening and paying attention to whoever interacts with you. You model the things you write about. For those who might still struggle with what it means to care, they have to look no further than you for ways you embody caring in practice.

As my focus shifted to the case at hand, and since I knew that you were also going to write, I challenged myself to do my best in my responses. I consider the two pieces (response to the case, and then thinking with you about the case) as some of my finest writings. What an honor it has been!

Now, to the case. It gave me further insight into your notion of care. The case was about a high school math teacher, Lucy Williams, who had taught for 23 years, and her ethical dilemma related to implementation of a testing policy that she had serious objections to. And, as all of life often poses challenges, this was complicated by other factors that Lucy needed to take into account: One was having a new African American principal with whom she had loyalties, being herself African American, and another was needing to work to support her children's college education. For Lucy, concepts of "self" and "moral integrity" were very important. But she also cared about others. You and I had to sort through and guide Lucy on what action she ought to take: whether to leave her school district or stay, and if she did the latter then under what circumstances.

Thinking with you about the case clarified the place that a teacher's unique sense of self might have in ways she examines her ethical world. And while we did not necessarily agree about the perceived role of duty in decision making or about what exactly it would mean to Lucy to "compromise" her ethical positions by staying, we actually had more agreements about caring for others even as the self tries to weigh the various ethical dilemmas. Once the book was published, I used the case and our responses to it in the classes I taught. I was intrigued to see how students weighed Lucy's dilemma and appeared fascinated with the approaches you and I had each taken to address it. Our thinking became transparent and itself served as an open book worthy of consideration; students were intently listening to our reasoning. This nudged them to think and pose questions. This kind of "thinking and listening" based on exposure to philosophers' reasoning is missing in much of our texts, from our schools, and also from public discourse altogether. Perhaps we need a book that takes various concrete education policy issues as "cases" and crafts out a similar approach taken by Hostetler—inviting philosophers of education to address the policy problems we presently confront.

I have also used your book *The Challenge to Care in Schools* (1992) in my philosophy of education classes for several years. The book speaks to every student, whether they are interested in K–12 schools or in working from the outside. As an elected official on the Portland School Board since 2003, I am keenly aware of the enormity of our school problems. However, whether we have No Child Left Behind or Race to the Top, we are still caught in the same educational paradigm devoid of "care." Caring cannot be achieved by "formula," as you argue; plus, we need constancy in people, place, purpose, and curriculum, as you rightly point out. These challenges notwithstanding, I am afraid that your urgings for engrossment, modeling, dialogue, and confirmation as requirements for "care" have not been heeded by the decision makers. As an educational policy maker, I continue to be dismayed by the misguided norms of control hammering away at public schools in the name of accountability. We see decisions made from the top, in central district offices, by outside foundations and agencies, prescribing the what, when, to what degree, and in what way every child and youth must learn specified content in preparation for tests. Contrary to an ethic of care, narrowly defined disciplines and narrow forms of rationality are seen as hallmarks of a full life. Unlike Dewey, for whom education *is* life, our national policies construe education as "preparation" for college or a career after schooling. These policies also glorify "expert" knowledge that favors linguistic and mathematical capacities, often undervaluing skills, attitudes, and capacities that are traditionally associated with women, as you argue. When we value the work of women, when we value the work of the teacher, and when we honor and build on the interest of each child to make education relevant for students, we provide conditions for them to care about what they are learning.

And, finally, I could never thank you enough for sponsoring me as visiting professor at Stanford when you were dean, during my sabbatical year in 1996–1997. Your support helped me to stay engaged intellectually and finish my manuscript for a coedited book, *Ecological Education in Action: On Weaving Education, Culture, and the Environment* (Smith & Williams, 1999). Those months at Stanford also solidified my admiration for you: a quiet but thoughtful administrator, a caring educator, a warm and wise human being. Inviting me to your home, where we met several of your doctoral students and engaged in rich dialogue, further reiterated for me that the personal and the professional Nel Noddings cannot be separated, that the philosopher and the mother and wife are one and the same, and that the teacher and the mentor reinforce each other. Solace, calm, dignity, and human decency cannot be compromised, since we are always in dialogue with the other as we clarify ideas and thoughts, arguments, and positions. I can only say this, without hesitation: You, Nel Noddings, are an embodiment of care and caring in practice.

Sincerely,

Dilafruz Williams

Toward an Education That Is Moral: Learning from/with Nel

Tianlong Yu

Dear Nel,

I am delighted to write this letter and attempt to express my great fortune for having known you and the immeasurable benefit your mentoring has had on my life and career.

Of course I knew you long before you knew me. Years ago in China when I was a graduate student, I became interested in American educational theories, especially theories of moral education. You were already a recognized pioneer in the field. I studied your caring approach to moral education along with values clarification, Kolbergian cognitive developmentalism, and character education. As I delved into more of your work, I learned that your scholarly contribution is far beyond the area of moral education. I was also fascinated by aspects of your personal life that became public. Learning that you raised ten kids enthralled us, who were so used to a shrinking family size in China because of the one-child policy. It occurred to me that your exuberance in scholarship is consistent with your generous embrace of a very large family. Perhaps your expertise in care ethics and education flows from the myriad opportunities for caring that parenting such a large family requires!

You had become this legendary figure in my young mind, and I did imagine that one day I would meet you in person. However, I could scarcely have dared to dream that I would have you as my dissertation committee member, translate your book, and work with you on publications. It was the late 1990s when I left Beijing for upstate New York to pursue a doctorate. In the spring of 1999, you were invited to lecture at my school and it was there that we met. During the discussion, I asked you about the social construction of morality and moral education in schools. You praised me for raising a great question and gave careful analysis on the issue. That brief question-and-answer session left such an important mark on my thinking: I decided to further tackle the topic with my dissertation. I also remember you used examples from mathematics to explain other education issues. Although I didn't understand everything in the math examples, I was impressed by the way you taught us. You are certainly a gentle, thorough, encouraging, and most of all caring teacher.

The fact that you are so approachable sets you apart from many of your colleagues in academia. It was a high point in my life when you accepted my invitation to join my dissertation committee. The 2 years of the dissertation process turned out to be quite enjoyable for me, largely because of your being part of it. You helped me experience the excitement of the journey and satisfaction with my achievement. Your highly respected stature in education and philosophy gave me a sense of security but also inspired me to press forward. Although we didn't often get the chance to meet in person, I felt you were always standing by my side, waiting for my questions, watching me with warmth and wisdom. After I successfully defended my dissertation, you said to me, "Now you can think about turning your thesis into a book!" I followed your advice and did just that.

Since then I have continued to research and write on moral education. In my time teaching in social foundations of education, my approach to the study of moral education has been largely informed by a socio-cultural orientation. I am concerned primarily with the issues of voice, power, and access and how they play out in moral education policies. Still influenced by my personal experience as a student within the highly politicized and oppressive Chinese educational system, I can't help but emphasize the politics of moral education here in the United States. Even though you do not write directly on political issues, I find your overall thinking on moral education extremely relevant for my work. In a 2004 article we coauthored to introduce Chinese readers to the Chinese edition of *The Challenge to Care in Schools*, which I translated, you offer a succinct critique of the character education movement in the United States and emphasize how the caring approach you represent fundamentally differs from character education. Your words are sharp: "[Character education] often supposes that there is something that must be done to kids to make them moral, while caring supposes that something must be done to the environment to make moral living both desirable and possible." (Noddings & Yu, 2004, p. 41). You clearly argue that building conditions and relationships that support moral ways of life is more important than inculcating virtues in students. Thus, you move caring from an admirable trait of individual character to a necessary cultural condition. Such a caring condition must be created throughout various relationships within a child's life, such as the relationships between the child and his or her family, teachers, and peers and the subject matter in schools and the larger environment.

Following your lead, I have argued in my book (Yu, 2004) that meaningful moral education requires school restructuring. Schooling today in many places is countering child development in general and moral development in particular. Poverty, racism, and the resulting "savage inequalities" (Kozol, 1992) are prevailing in so many schools, damaging numerous disadvantaged kids. A school system like those Kozol visited is morally deplorable; imposing a moral education program upon the dispossessed children that aims to make them moral and virtuous is hypocritical and only exacerbates social inequalities. Other school practices need to be critically examined as well, from a moral perspective. These include the differential and often racially charged tracking system, the dehumanizing zero-tolerance policies, and standardized, high-stakes tests, among others. Those of us concerned with moral education must first challenge these practices and help make the entire school culture morally defensible. It is so counterproductive to attempt to foster moral development in an institution where children's worth is assessed on a 4-point scale. Students see right through the hypocrisy here, even when they cannot yet articulate it. Education is not about sending everyone to the same destination. The human person cannot be codified, digitized, categorized, or statistically analyzed, and our schools should stop attempting to do this. What we should do is provide unconditional positive regard for our students as they achieve their personal best, whatever that may be.

I see a need to redefine moral education at this historical moment. Those of us busy with inventing new approaches, models, theories, or ideas that aim to fix the kids, not the environment, may want to take a break. It is time for us to work together to create and sustain an environment that allows the moral life to flourish. It is my not-so-wild imagination that if we had a moral school where the child's moral character is adequately nurtured and fostered, we would not need any separate, additive moral education programs. Indeed, *all* education should occur under the umbrella of morality, not alongside it. You made clear as early as 1992 that too often we view moral education as a subset of education aiming to teach children how to be moral, but we would do better to devote ourselves to "an education that is moral in purpose, policy, and methods" (Noddings, 1992, p. xiii). Yes, let's strive for an education that is moral. This is what John Dewey taught us over a century ago, as you repeatedly reminded us. I agree that we still have a long way to go. And, thank you, Nel, for being my inspiration on this journey!

Sincerely,

Tian Yu

CHAPTER 4

A Circle of Friends

Nel has written in several places about Aristotle's notion of friendship. Here is an excerpt from "A Morally Defensible Mission for Schools in the 21st Century" (2006b).

> Aristotle is one philosopher who wrote eloquently on friendship, and he assessed it as central in moral life. In the Nicomachean Ethics (trans. 1985), Aristotle wrote that the main criterion of friendship is that a friend wishes a friend well for her own sake. When we befriend others, we want good things for them not because those things may enhance our welfare but because they are good for our friends. Aristotle organized friendships into various categories: those motivated by common business or political purposes, those maintained by common recreational interests, and those created by mutual admiration of the other's virtue. The last was, for Aristotle, the highest form of friendship and, of course, the one most likely to endure. (p. 44)

At a time when mentoring is often relegated to the language of professional business relationships, where it is often graded with a bi-directional rubric, the letters below reinforce the immense value of circles of care, trust, and friendship within the academy and in and out of the classroom.

Our Lives at Stanford

Denis C. Phillips

Dear Nel,

This is the first time in our long relationship that I have written you a letter, and it is proving to be very difficult. Not counting the many social occasions that, along with Jim and Val, we enjoyed as couples together, you and I have of course interacted professionally face to face many hundreds if not thousands of times, and have exchanged memoranda and emails about students and courses, and we have given each other feedback on drafts of our research writings in which we have drawn attention to each other's philosophical foibles and possible deficiencies. It seems to me that I wrote more than you did! (You thanked me, in your great book *Caring,* for the detailed comments I had provided—but I wonder if you recall that in a later book, the draft of which had become available while I was out of touch overseas, you thanked me for *not* commenting!) Only good friends can be so forthright.

But now I am struggling—for how can a mere letter capture a stream of wonderful interactions that goes back for well over 3 decades? The task is so daunting I think I need to abandon all attempts to produce a coherent piece and settle, instead, for a series of vignettes—events that are alive in my memory and that hopefully will relive in yours.

I arrived at Stanford from Australia as an associate professor, at the start of the 1974–1975 academic year, but we did not meet, as you recently had graduated with your Ph.D. and had moved on. But over the next year or two your name cropped up from time to time; evidently you had taken courses in the philosophy department with Julius Moravcik, who had also served on your dissertation committee. He had so enjoyed the experience that he willingly served on the committee of one of my first students at Stanford (Glen Harvey). My image of you was shaped less by Julius's commendatory remarks than by the fact that he was a real "character" whose philosophical acumen sometimes was offset by a proclivity to put forward genuinely bizarre ideas that seem to have come from "left field." I thought there was a fair chance then that you, too, would be—to put it obliquely—something of an "outlier"! It turned out, however, that it was the other side of Julius's nature that was responsible for his high opinion of you.

We must have met at the Philosophy of Education Society conferences, but nothing stands out in my mind until—several years after my arrival at Stanford—the Noddings family moved back to the Stanford area from Chicago (where you had been head of the Dewey School at the University of Chicago). You started to work as a researcher for Pat Suppes, who in addition to his busy life as a professor in three or four Stanford departments (philosophy and education included), had found time to start a computer-based learning company and I guess it was your expertise as a math educator rather than your training in philosophy that made you valuable to him. But as luck would have it, our school of education had needs especially in the curriculum and teacher education areas (I vaguely recall that Elliot Eisner went on sabbatical) and so you started to work part-time for us; eventually we had the opportunity—and the good sense—to appoint you full-time. Around the mid-1980s the young colleague who worked with me in philosophy of education failed to obtain tenure, and you moved into that billet.

My first impressions of you as a colleague in the late 1970s and early 1980s were that you were an exceptionally experienced math educator who was also an extremely competent analytic philosopher who, like many of us at the time, produced no doubt important but extremely dry (if not completely arid) papers on what then were standard topics in our field—such things as the "task" versus "achievement" senses of "teaching" and "educating," the differences between teaching, educating, and indoctrinating . . . Blessedly I have actually forgotten not only the precise topics within this genre that you wrote on, but also the topics that I contributed to. But clearly this commonality in analytic training allowed us to communicate easily, and we also had a bond in our mutual interest in John Dewey. But then . . . ! I watched in awe as you made a quantum leap and produced a series of remarkable books, starting with *Caring*.

Several instances involving our teaching stand out. A couple of times we jointly ran a seminar series on Dewey for our advanced students, and following what was then still something of a Stanford tradition (now, I think, completely dead), we taught it in the evenings at our own homes. I recall one series of meetings held in your lounge room, with about a dozen students in easy chairs or on pillows beside the fire; typically each session would start with both of us drawing attention to a couple of passages from the first of the assigned passages (from a chapter of *Democracy and Education*, for example) that we regarded as especially significant, and after we had made some points about these the students would take turns highlighting passages that they wanted to discuss. What struck me forcibly was that the two of us rarely, if ever, had selected the same passages as worthy of note (even from the one chapter). Almost invariably you chose passages that were pedagogically rich, while my focus seemed always to be on passages of philosophical significance or where I felt Dewey's argument was philosophically dubious in some way. Whatever the excerpt, however, there always was lively discussion. (On several occasions a visiting scholar from overseas attended, and in later years a couple of them told me how memorable those seminars remained for them.)

Then, of course, there was that extraordinary afternoon when you invited our colleague Myra Strober to be a guest lecturer in the 1st hour of your class, but you also arranged for her to be wearing a pants suit. Then I came for the 2nd hour, but wearing—as you had requested—a simple dress, about which I was not to make any remark. (Actually, I wore a plain gray dress, a black polo-neck shirt with a simple gold chain, and black socks and shoes. Rather fetching!) After I had made my presentation and had left, you debriefed the class; no one commented on the fact that Myra had dressed in typical male clothing, but of course everyone noticed my attire. A few students said they had not known that I was Scottish (evidently they thought I must be wearing the Phillips clan kilt!), but most thought I was offering a satirical challenge to you, the feminist, or at least playing an insulting prank. Subsequent discussion opened the issue of why it was acceptable for a member of a less socially dominant group to "dress up," but not acceptable for a member of the dominant group to "dress down."

Myra's reputation remained unsullied by this event, but it took me several years to live it down!

In subsequent years, while we remained close colleagues at Stanford, our professional lives seemed to run in parallel. I became president of the Philosophy of Education Society, and you followed the next year; you served as interim dean of Sanford's school of education, and several years later I followed suit (but for a shorter period); and we both became members of the U.S. National Academy of Education—and you performed marvelous service as its president. Sadly, however, neither of us has sold the film rights to any of our books (personally, I still live in hope). I have also thought that it would be a fitting tribute to you if, in a film or TV bio, the role of Nel Noddings was played by Meryl Streep or perhaps Dame Judi Dench. I would be happy if the minor supporting role of Denis C. Phillips was played by Dustin Hoffman; and of course the role of the leading man—Jim—would be a suitable challenge for Harrison Ford.

At any rate, thanks for the memories.

Denis Phillips

The Day You Intervened

Liora Bresler

Dear Nel,

Spring 1983. Yours was the very first course I took at Stanford. Recruited by Elliot for a research project, bright eyed, musically trained, and new to the world of education. Your course was recommended warmly and enthusiastically by everybody I talked with. Indeed, coupled with Elliot's course Aesthetic Foundations of Education, it was a compelling introduction to the world of ideas whose vibrancy and depth matched those provided by the arts.

There were the readings, many of which I returned to 20 years later—*I and Thou* by Martin Buber (1970), *Becoming* by Gordon Allport (1955), and a whole array of others, that shaped my thinking and being, providing me with a glimpse of what scholarship could be. Not less important was the feeling of collegiality, of caring about the implications of ideas to live the good and wise life.

I learned in your course one of the most important lessons in my life. It was in the final projects. I have just finished my own project-presentation, where we all went to the Tressider building, the one that had a piano. I talked about music as both supporting individualization and creating a community, and played a Beethoven piano sonata (more nervous than in a formal concert) to illustrate the former, and folk songs to illustrate the latter (not fully acknowledging the interconnections of these).

The presentation after mine was by a student in educational psychology (that's what I believe her major is). Back to Cubberly, we descended to the basement, where the presenter arranged the chairs and asked for a volunteer for her experiment. The volunteer had her eyes blindfolded. The experimenter asked the volunteer to walk around the room among the labyrinth of chairs, guided by our directions on how to navigate. Suddenly, the experimenter motioned us to be quiet, and the directions stopped. The blindfolded student halted, not knowing where to proceed. I remember what I perceived as her distress. And I remember my conflict—wanting to step in to help, then stepping back, worrying about me, a novice, disrupting a Stanford experience. After what felt like a long time, but must have been less than a minute, you stepped in. You held the volunteer's hand, saying in your even, measured, calming tone, "I don't know what the purpose of this experiment is, but I would betray my role as a teacher and a person if I did not intervene."

I learned then that no matter how inexperienced, I should intervene when something that did not feel right is happening.

Your presence in my doctoral committee had the same centered, moral stance that I found enormously important, more fundamental than any scholarship, any achievement. These were all part of the same thing, knowing that scholarship was about becoming more human, talking about things that are important to us, mind and spirit, that touch us, that help us become even more who we want to become. I am grateful for many things at Stanford, but I recognize that it was this message that propelled me to become a researcher.

When, more than 20 years later, I embarked on a project of the *Handbook of Research in Arts Education*, with 100-plus scholars in the arts, I knew the book wouldn't be complete without you there. I was thinking of you as epitomizing the art of the wise, moral, generous life. Your chapter, "Interlude: War, Violence, and Peace in the Arts" in the *Handbook*, addressing peace education, epitomized these qualities.

—Liora

The Carer and the Cared For

Sara Ruddick

Dear Nel,

I was pretty well set to write my short "letter" when Joan Callahan sent me a copy on a DVD of the high-spirited interview she and Nancy Tuana recorded with you for their series of interviews titled *Feminist Philosophers: In Their Own Words* (Callahan & Tuana, 2008). Your interview gave me a clearer, livelier understanding of your work.

Since you and I may be the only readers who can hear the tape, let alone see the DVD, I decided to make a shortened written version of the interview that I could then allude to, and all readers could share. I must emphasize that this is not a transcription but a narrative of my own that I have attempted to base closely on your words. A nearly literal transcript would be beyond my skill or endurance.

The Interview

You began your interview with Nancy and Joan by answering the question, Where were you born? You hardly had time to speak the words—Irvington, New Jersey—before telling us how you could know that the elementary school you attended as a small child, the Brookdale School in Bloomfield, New Jersey, was "progressive" and generally marvelous. You then tell us about the imaginary walks you still take through the landscapes of your childhood, describing them and naming individual bushes and trees. These now inspire your recent explorations of "place-based education to preserve the earth and its people" and less formally the "countless different ways that place shapes us" (Noddings, 2002, p. 152).

With remarkable openness you then spoke about becoming detached from your family around the age of 7. You liked them, they liked you, but your emotional life was centered in school. This is why you talked about school when asked about your childhood. Indeed you do seem "embedded" in school as a student, teacher, principal, policy maker, colleague, and writer. Yet you are also attached to another "home" that you mention but only rarely describe. You dedicate *Caring* (Noddings, 2003a), your first book, to your husband, whom you married when you were both 20. You dedicated *Women and Evil* (Noddings, 1989), your second book, to your five daughters and five sons.

During the course of the interview you told two stories about how you came to the idea of writing about caring. "How did this get started?" you ask your interviewers as you begin your first story. You remember explicitly, in a way unusual for you, "sitting myself down" and "asking myself" how I could bring together the two parts of my life. At the time you experienced this division, the two parts were "high powered" analytic philosophy and philosophy of education as taught at Stanford University and your work teaching and mothering ten children at various ages and places in their lives. One way you brought the two parts of yourself together was to write "quite an analytical" paper on care and then deliver it at a meeting of a professional association that was publicly insistent on rigor.

Was writing about care a unifying action? Did a "soft analytic" style of argument, and frequent allusion to other analytic philosophers, temper the division? (I am describing your way of doing "analytic" philosophy today.) Were you, as you lectured, becoming at once a philosopher and a teacher-and-mother? (The latter two already bracketed together for you.) Or is there still a division between the rigorous systematizing philosopher and the angry mother-teacher who believes that "our public schools are under siege," prey to a system that is "terrifyingly anti-intellectual and anti democratic." I ask because I barely guessed at the existence of an angry, public-speaking, politically committed mother-teacher—though she was there to know. Does the politically engaged mother-teacher's audience know of your work in phenomenology and the ethics of care?

The second story you tell about the origins of your dedication to the ethic of caring took place both earlier and later than the healing of self-division. In part 1 you are living in a school district that is overcrowded and understaffed. You were given an emergency credential that allowed you to teach 6th grade in an elementary school. As it turned out you were thrilled by the teaching, especially the opportunity to revisit the "literature of childhood" that you had loved and to teach the history of Greece, Rome, and Egypt. Most important, since the school continued to be overcrowded, you were able to teach a 2nd and then a 3rd year with the same students.

After working at Stanford for over 20 years you came back to the East Coast. Some of the students you had taught for 3 continuous years before moving out west arranged a reunion. The whole town and its officials seem to have attended. In the toasts and speeches you heard how much the 3 years spent together had meant to "the kids," the students now nearly ready to retire. You were especially moved by the man who had served as master of ceremonies for the evening and who at the finish stretched out his arms and said, "I love you guys." "Is that an outcome you would want from your teaching?" you ask the audience of the DVD (Callahan & Tuana, 2008)? "Or do you want to make sure they know their quadratic equations?" You had always known what those years meant to you but you had not known that they had meant so much to the "kids." It was this discovery that led you to say in your speech to the group, "This is where, for me, the ethic of caring began. Right here, in this school, with you."

Close to the end of the interview, into the present century, you accuse the George W. Bush administration of making a "No Child Left Behind" law that is coercive, ignorant, and, implicitly, cruel to children. You and some colleagues were organizing political resistance to this law at the time of the interview. At the least your eloquent anger should clear a path to the alternative education you believe is "permissible in the 21st century," one whose aim is to "encourage the growth of competent, caring, loving and lovable people." This is a constant theme in your scholarship. I will mention two of your perhaps lesser-known books as examples.

In *Women and Evil* (Noddings, 1989), your claims about the "feminine" become hermeneutically layered (p. 144). The idea of a "feminine" perspective "is a *conceptual creation* that is in part derived from the experiences of real women, in part created by the ritualized expectations of a culture." We who are reading your latest book might say that in this culture we expect of mothers, and we also observe in mothers, a fierce love of their children and an ability to "read" their infants that emerges out of that love. In *Women and Evil* (Noddings, 1989) I found your description of the activities and reflections ascribed to women especially affecting, perhaps because they were set against the evils of pain, separation, and helplessness. But as in *Caring* (Noddings, 2003a) you strike a note of openness and caution regarding differences between men and women. "We don't yet have the evidence that would let us say that women more than men had skills and interests in caring (Noddings, 1989, p. 136). Finally, in the interview you continue to advocate waiting on the evidence before making strong statements either affirming or denying sex/gender differences.

In *The Maternal Factor* (Noddings, 2010) there is a change. You are confident that women and men differ in their approaches to relationships, that the differences go beyond socialization, and that at least some of the differences can be traced to biological evolution. Then you introduce a Difference that organizes differences. Characteristics associated with masculinity are, just because of that association, held in higher esteem than allegedly feminine or female characteristics. Conversely, whatever is characterized as "female" is lesser than what is characterized as "male." Or so feminists, I included, have argued. Yet I wonder. It seems that when we—you and I—read and write about what we call "feminine," we are often trying to bring into speech what we love. When you hunt down evolutionary legacies associated with "male" tendencies we look for characteristics that are "too dangerous for the health of humanity and must be transformed" (p. 222). I wanted to remind myself that it was tendencies toward domination, aggression, and violence you would want to undermine whether or not they were, as you believe, male and masculine.

In a skeptical mood I began to read you side by side with Virginia Woolf. I was struck by similarities I didn't anticipate and then by the differences that attention to similarities could reveal. In her war-rejecting polemic, *Three Guineas* (1963), Virginia Woolf imagined a "transformed curriculum" within a new college:

> You must rebuild your college differently . . . on lines of its own. . . . It should teach the arts of human intercourse; the art of understanding other people's lives and minds . . . and the little arts of talk and dress and cookery that are allied with them. . . . It should explore the ways in which mind and body can

be made to cooperate; discover what new combinations make good wholes in human lives. (p. 43)

In 1940, while war was under way and bombing overhead, Virginia Woolf asked a friend to "think about sharing life after the war: about pooling men's and women's work; about the possibility, if disarmament comes, of removing men's disabilities. How can we alter the crest and the spur of the fighting cock?" (Letter #3580, 1980).

I am still reading you and Virginia Woolf side by side, seeing each of you differently in the light of the other. This comparative reading cannot be a letter. It is frankly an essay in the making. I sift through the pages of your books, noting passages that I have underlined. Your achievement is massive, your ambition precise: to "infuse caregiving, diplomacy, global interaction, and family practices with an appreciation of the attitudes, skills, and understandings that are described in care ethics" (Noddings, 2010, p. 249). Your project asks for attention, for response, for the "critical thinking" that care requires (p. 243). But I must end this letter. I will close where care ethics begins—in the call and response of an intimate encounter (adapted from Noddings, 2002, p. 128).

The 1st days and weeks of caregiving should establish a caring relation. Because the child and its response are fundamental to a caring relation, that response must be "elicited and treasured" from the very first.

I am here, said by a parent to a child, is an offering of love that flows downward from those with greater power to those with less.

You are there. This is a child's recognition of the parent's offering of love. "The child gains her first sense of her own existence from the mother's responsive gestures and expressions. It's as if, in the mother's eyes, her smile, her stroking touch, the child first reads the message:

You are there (A. Rich, cited in Noddings, 2002, p. 128)

You are there! This is the child's inner reaction to the parent's assurance.

I am here. The constant response "I am here" is the "foundation of a relation of care and trust." Projected onto the social scene, it represents the assurance that every community should offer its members in a time of need.

A reminder: You needn't be a parent to be affected by what happens at home. ***Every person started life at home, however various homes might be.***

—Sara

I Still Have Need for Your Company

Pradeep Dhillion

Dear Nel,

Perhaps it is impossible to write any letter without engaging affect and reason. In writing to you, however, their play is brought to the fore—not only in acknowledging your work, but also in appreciation of the kinds of relationships you fostered with all those who were fortunate enough to have known you. There is only one other person, that I know, who has that kind of effect on all who come in contact with her—my lovely and gracious mother. While she lived a circumscribed life, she, like you, taught through both discourse and personal example, that we must cherish the lives, our own and those of others, that constitute the worlds we inhabit.

I came to your classes—that first semester I was at Stanford, alone and far from home and everything that was familiar. The transition was one that brought me not only from India to the United States but also from the drawing room to the classroom. I was lost. The hours in your class, however, were pure joy, providing, as they did, a complete commitment to intellectual work in a manner that all awareness of constraints fell away. This was true even of the early morning course on critical thinking that, for some reason, you chose to teach during winter quarter. I would ride my bicycle in the freezing rain as I hurried to an hour spent with truth tables and exercises in logical thinking, as well as discussions regarding the value and limits of this mode of reasoning. That I loved these exercises amused and pleased you—but what I never told you is that I delighted in practicing my scales when I was learning music. I found beauty in the patterns and progressions they carried. It is not surprising to me now, as I look back, that you encouraged me in my study of theoretical linguistics, fostering rigor in thinking even as you encouraged philosophical exploration of the human heart. Again, standing close to the liberal theories that you cherished, you never once held me back from my deepening engagement with Kantian thought—except to say, "That old grouch!" In so doing, you taught me to step away from more Byronic modes of philosophizing to doing so in a voice that was, as the poet Mary Kinzie so movingly reminds us, more modest, though no less fierce and clear, for all its being small.

You sent me the first edition of your book laying out your theory of care while I was doing fieldwork in Delhi during the troubled year of 1984. I would read passages from your book and reflect on the ways it squared—and did not—with the opening lines of Richard Fariña's poem "Children of Darkness" sung hauntingly by Joan Baez (Farina, 1966). Amid the escalating circle of violence, I longed for the oak tables, high ceilings, and tall windows bringing in the late afternoon sun, as our classroom filled with the sound of your calm voice:

> Oh, now is the time for your loving, dear,
> And time for your company
> Now when the light of reason fails
> And fires burn on the sea
> Oh, now in this age of confusion.

The cover of the book was yellow, with a photograph of a young family. That cover disappeared, to be replaced by the pink cover that is now associated with your groundbreaking book. You shrugged off my indignation at the stereotyping reproduced by the book's front cover and the reference to you as Mrs. Noddings on the back. It could be said that perhaps some of the misrepresentations of your theoretical positions can be laid at the door of those pink covers and their 19th-century aesthetic that signals a sentimentality of thought to those too hurried to read what lies between.

Clearly, I have been much influenced by your theories, as I have your person. Caring, you would remind us, is a reciprocal relationship. I hope that you always knew that your concern was, and is, reciprocated deeply by your students as we work in the field you carved out for us. I close, then, with Emily Dickinson's reflections on the modest efforts that go into the making of the great prairie:

> It's all I have to bring today–
> This, and my heart beside–
> This, and my heart, and all the fields–
> And all the meadows wide–
> Be sure you count–should I forget
> Some one the sum could tell–
> This, and my heart, and all the Bees
> Which in the clover dwell.
> (1960, p. 18)

Warm regards,

Pradeep

Nel Noddings, A Pioneer for Caring in Education, Social Theory, and Life: A Letter of Admiration and Appreciation

Riane Eisler

Dear Nel,

I want to congratulate you on your birthday, and tell you how much your work on caring and your own caring have meant to me, how important these have been for me personally and in the development of my own thinking and writing.

I am of course not the only one so affected. Your work, through books such as *Caring: A Feminine Approach to Ethics and Moral Education* (2003a) and *The Challenge to Care in Schools: An Alternative Approach to Education* (1992), have influenced many fields, from philosophy to education.

Perhaps the most notable aspect of your contribution to philosophy and moral theory is that your germinal concept of ethical caring adds a much needed "soft," stereotypically feminine voice to philosophical and moral discourse. Rather than focusing on ethical abstractions, your work recognizes our deep human need for caring connection and postulates its fulfillment as a key component of ethical relations.

As for your enormous contributions to education, your focus on caring in education has greatly advanced the field by recognizing the seemingly obvious, but still largely ignored, fact that children (and adults) learn best not only when they feel cared for but also when they are inspired to care about what they are studying.

In these and other writings, you have played a major role in legitimizing the use of terms such as *caring* in academia, showing its vital role in all aspects of our lives. For this in itself, we all owe you a major debt of gratitude.

This takes me to my own personal and professional debt of gratitude to you. To say that I was thrilled when you wrote the foreword to my own book on education, *Tomorrow's Children: A Blueprint for Partnership Education in the 21st Century* (Eisler, 2000), is an understatement. That you took the time out of your busy schedule to do this was a huge gift to me. When you later agreed to do the foreword to another book, *Educating for a Culture of Peace* (which I coedited with Ron Miller; Eisler & Miller, 2004), I was again thrilled by your generous support. Indeed, I cannot adequately express how much all this means to me.

But your contribution to my own work goes deeper and further. Indeed, caring is a thread that runs through my work, through all my writings.

You may recall, for example, that in *Tomorrow's Children* I propose that caring for life—for self, for others, and for our Mother Earth—be part of the curriculum from preschool to graduate school.

Even before then, in my *The Chalice and the Blade: Our History, Our Future*, caring is a major theme. As you know, this book, which you have kindly praised, introduces the partnership model and the domination model as two underlying human possibilities for structuring beliefs, institutions, and relationships—from intimate to international. It shows the connection between the subordination of the female half of humanity and the devaluation of caring, caregiving, nonviolence, and other traits and activities stereotypically considered "feminine" in societies that orient to a domination rather than partnership model. And it calls for the reinstatement of these values as guiding principles not only for morality and spirituality but also for social and economic policy.

My next book, *Sacred Pleasure: Sex, Myth, and the Politics of the Body*, takes your theme of fulfilling our deep human need for caring connection into the relations that are still ignored in much of the spiritual literature: our intimate sexual relations. It calls for an ethic for intimate relations no longer based on the moralistic dominator tenets of control that have caused so much suffering, particularly to women and girls, who are still in some world regions basically the sexual property of men, but on a partnership morality based on caring, mutual respect, and mutual accountability.

Caring is also a key theme in the book I wrote after *Tomorrow's Children*, *The Power of Partnership: Seven Relationships That Can Change Your Life*. This is a different kind of self-help book that calls for caring practices and policies as basic to healthier, more equitable, more fulfilling relationships—as well as to full human development.

As you know, my most recent book, in which you are of course also cited, is *The Real Wealth of Nations*. Its subtitle, *Creating a Caring Economics*, says it all. This book shows that to move to a more equitable, sustainable, and effective economic system, real visibility and value must be given to the most important human work: caring for people, starting in early childhood, and caring for our natural environment. It is replete with data demonstrating that, contrary to what is indicated by the popular dismissal of caring and caregiving as economically ineffective, caring and caregiving have enormous payoff not only in human and environmental terms but also in purely financial terms.

In these and other ways I am following in your footsteps, Nel, showing, as you put it, that "there is nothing mushy about caring. It is the strong resilient backbone of human life."

So I want to again thank you for all your contributions: to me personally and to your students, colleagues, and readers—to us all. As you have powerfully shown, our capacity to care is basic to what makes us human—and therefore must be developed in us from childhood on if we are to build that better world we all so want and need.

Congratulations, dear Nel, on your birthday and for all you have done and are doing to help make ours that better, more caring, world.

With admiration and affection,

Riane Eisler

Profound Generosity

Madeleine Grumet

Dear Nel,

It is a little strange to write a letter to you in this public text when that has not been the way we have communicated over the decades. We were always grabbing a few minutes in hotel lobbies and academic receptions, introducing our spouses or children, if we were lucky enough to have them with us, sustaining an intimacy that was intermittent and compelling. Except for the lovely evening I spent with you and your family in your home while you were still at Stanford, our friendship has been subordinated to our schedules, our responsibilities, and our ambitions.

And so we have not shared the kind of intimacy that grows when women live in the same neighborhood, sharing kids, carpools, early morning walks, local gossip. Nevertheless, the sense that we know each other well endures, and it is because we share this work that we do. Through your work I discern your warmth and your toughness, your impulses and your subtlety. And through our work together we have shared the project of making educational institutions places that encourage presence, engagement, and growth.

I cannot remember a time that we met when you did not tell me that you were involved in a new project that was fascinating to you, and the range of your mind and topics that engaged you is astonishing. Your energy and accomplishments make the term *overextended* the caution of a stingy mind. It has seemed that with every effort, you have flourished, enriched with each investment, having more and more to offer. Your work on caring that challenged and guided educators across the globe is propelled by this generosity. And in your texts readers find the confidence to extend, to be their more interested, more attentive, more active selves.

I think that what I am trying to say is that your work is a gesture that expresses a spirit that is both contained in, yet transcends, the context of its speaking. What I celebrate in you is this profound generosity and the encouragement it provides to your readers, your students, and your friends.

Until we meet again, in some corridor or airport,

I am your devoted friend,

Madeleine

Thanks for Your Support, Modeling, and Scholarship

James G. Henderson

Nel,

I write my letter in a personal tone and from the heart because I think this approach best conveys my feelings about how you have added value to my life and to the education profession. As I considered how to compose my thank you, I realized that, given your scholarly productivity, I could easily write an academic essay with 50 citations. However, such an approach felt too pedantic and sterile, particularly in light of the *deep humanism* that infuses your impressive body of work. As I reflected back on my 30-year higher education career, I realized that I felt grateful to you in three specific ways: for your caring support at a critical point in my doctoral studies, for your inspirational modeling as an educational scholar, and for your many intellectual contributions. My letter is a personal expression of this threefold sense of gratitude.

I begin with my doctoral studies. In the fall of 1979, I confronted a major obstacle in completing and successfully defending my dissertation and felt doubly challenged because my major advisor, Elliot Eisner, was going to spend the 1979–1980 academic year in England. This was in pre-Internet days, and I wondered how I was going to regularly communicate with him. Elliot and I came up with a solution that involved your caring support. Assuming that you were willing, you would serve as my de facto advisor in Elliot's absence, and I would share my completed dissertation with him when he returned in June 1980. You agreed; the strategy worked smoothly, and I was able to successfully defend my dissertation in July 1980. We met regularly during the 1979–1980 academic year, and I always came away from our meetings feeling inspired, energized, and affirmed. You completed your book on an ethic of caring a few years later; and as I read this text, I realized that I was very fortunate to have had such a personal, hands-on experience with your notions of confirmation, dialogue, and practice. You embody what you argue and advance. There is no inconsistency between what you write and how you act. I applaud you for your ethical fidelity, which, at times, feels like a rare commodity in higher education.

I also feel grateful for the way you have integrated generative, critical, practical, and personal perspectives into your scholarship. You have been an inspirational model to me in this way, and I begin with a brief summation of my own career and then turn to your *Philosophy of Education* (1998a) text. In the early 1980s, I began to think about how to advance a conception of "reflective teaching" that would be informed by the "reconceptualization" of curriculum studies that was under way. As I worked on that topic, I realized that the reflective teachers who interested me would, necessarily, have to work as transformative curriculum leaders in the United States' highly managed educational systems. This entire line of inquiry generated a number of scholarly products, including three editions of a reflective teaching book and three editions of a coauthored curriculum leadership book.

As I proceeded with my research trajectory, I did my best to incorporate generative, critical, practical, and personal insights into my scholarship. I wanted to avoid critical work that was overly ideological and narcissistic (Pinar, 2009) and, thus, lacking in the generative, generous "for all" spirit that underlies democracy as the moral basis for living (Dewey, 1989). I wanted to avoid practical work that was narrowly technical and procedural and, thus, lacking in a deliberative commitment to eclectic, case-based decision-making (Schwab, 1971). Similarly, I wanted to avoid conceptions of practice that lacked a hermeneutic commitment to a deepening understanding of democratic education (Henderson & Kesson, 1999). In part, I was concerned about the pervasiveness of a vulgar pragmatism (Cherryholmes, 1988) that was disconnected from critical social theorizing with its multifaceted insights into unjust, hidden curricula (Apple, 1979). Finally, I wanted to avoid interpretations of educational practice that lacked existential insight. I agreed with Pinar and Grumet (1976) that there is much power in interpreting curriculum as *currere*–as the critically informed, personal running of an educational course of action; and I resonated with Greene's (1988) celebration of individual emancipatory journeys grounded in freedom from/to dialectics.

Nel, your philosophy text is a vivid illustration of the powerful synergy of the generative, critical, practical, and personal in educational scholarship. From one sentence, one paragraph, and one chapter to the next, you adeptly move *from* open-minded, philosophic questioning *to* critical social justice with a feminist emphasis *to* robust, pragmatic discussions and insights *to* broadly humanistic and personally caring affirmations. Your philosophy book is a wonderful symphony of historically significant, well-integrated intellectual currents and a powerful illustration of how a Socratic "love of wisdom" can be applied to educational studies (Henderson & Kesson, 2004).

I am currently engaged in the design and enactment of a pilot Teacher Leadership Endorsement Program (TLEP) for the state of Ohio. Ohio is currently at the policy forefront in mandating teacher leadership as a central feature of educational reform. I am working on the TLEP pilot with several educational colleagues, and the notion of *teachers working as 21st-century professional leaders* serves as our normative focus. We argue that management strategies are not designed to build teachers' intellectual capacities and that these top-down approaches often interfere with the sophisticated work of educational professionals. In essence, we make the critical point that the reform vision of fostering 21st-century student learning cannot be accomplished using the same thinking that created the current educational management realities. Based on this argument, we have designed a 4-course sequence that facilitates teacher leaders' disciplined learning through specific curriculum study applications of critical thinking, multidisciplinary inquiry, systemic deliberation, and disciplinary evaluation. The first course in our TLEP sequence is titled Curriculum Leadership; and Nel, your two texts *Philosophy of Education* (1998a) and *When School Reform Goes Wrong* (2007) are important intellectual resources for this course. Both books model and support the disciplined professionalism we are advancing.

Again, Nel, thanks so much for your support, your modeling, and your scholarship. You have contributed so much to the quality of my personal and professional life and to the education field as a whole. I'm forever grateful.

–James Henderson

Nel Noddings: Evolutionary Outrider

David Loye

Dear Nel,

This is an excerpt from my book *Revolution and Counter Revolution*, scheduled for publication later this year. It is the first volume of a trilogy, *Darwin and the Battle for 21st-Century Mind.* This sketch of you will appear in Chapter 12, "The Battle for Heart and Much Larger Mind," in which in similarly brief sketches I try to bring to life a dozen examples of "evolutionary outriders" in the fields of science, education, philosophy, and religion and the peace, environmental, and women's movements. You're also on the cover of the book—you can see it along with contents and advance excerpts on my website: www.davidloye.com.

Here's the context in which this sketch of you appears.

Politically and economically the battle for 21st century mind is shaping up as a social and environmental fight to the death between revolutionaries pushing for the freedom, equality, and *expansion* of mind and paradigm, and counter-revolutionaries pushing for the control, inequality, and a *diminishing* of mind and paradigm.

In *The Evolutionary Outrider: The Impact of the Human Agent on Evolution*, in 1998 I introduced the concept of the *evolutionary outrider*. The term was meant to capture the situation of those who boldly scout on ahead of us to explore potentially revolutionary as well as evolutionary prospects for a better future. These evolutionary outriders, I see now, are of two kinds.

One set is of the theorists, whose story we've tracked, who seek to better understand, and teach, and thereby help guide evolution scientifically or spiritually. The other group, however—orienting, although without knowing it, to the lost Darwinian half emphasizing love and moral sensitivity—simply set aside the often alien tangle of the theory part of it to listen to their hearts, and go ahead and work to advance evolution along the paths that come to seem obvious to them into the future. The history of our species further shows that frequently the activists lead the way for theory to follow.

The year was 1984. While somehow also managing the miracle of raising ten children, Stanford professor Nel Noddings had just published *Caring: A Feminine Approach to Ethics and Moral Education* (2003a). Behind her was the tradition of a morally oriented progressive education going back to Pestalozzi in 1801. Maria Montessori and John Dewey were among her treasured predecessors. Currently, Ron Miller, Tim Seldin, and others were probing the prospects for evolutionary advance in this direction.

Particularly in keeping with Darwin's and later Piaget's grounding in the parent-child relation for their understanding of the impact of education on evolution, Noddings had forged ahead to found a nationally influential perspective on all levels of education in the intimacy of family life.

"We should want more from our educational efforts than adequate academic achievement," she urged. "We will not achieve even that meager success unless our children believe that they themselves are cared for and learn to care for others.

> Caring parents and teachers provide the conditions in which it is possible and attractive for children to respond as carers to others. . . . Children educated in this way gradually build an ethical ideal, a dependable caring self. A society composed of people capable of caring—people who habitually draw on a well-established ideal—will move toward social policies consonant with an ethical care." (Noddings, 2002, p. 223)

—David Loye

A Weekend with Nel and Jim Noddings

James Marshall

Dear Nel,

First thank you both, once again, for your hospitality over the weekend, and Nel, the time you kindly gave me, away from your garden, leaving Jim in charge, to sort out some of the ideas that I had been "playing" with—mainly unsuccessfully, but with one major exception—the Self and the Other (in Simone de Beauvoir and Jean-Paul Sartre). It was a pity that Lynda (Stone—my wife) could not be with us as originally planned but, perhaps, that gave us a little more time to talk! Although I have known you since 1981, I did not know much at all of your pre-Stanford life and early experiences.

I would note from your early teaching experiences pedagogical traits that you carried forward, from teaching at Woodbury in Matawan. You taught a continuous group of 6th- to 9th-graders over those 3 years, not only maths, but everything. But that important pedagogical experience shaped your later approach to university students—both mentoring and caring (if they can be separated).

You followed a number of advanced courses in philosophy at Stanford as prerequisites for Ph.D. acceptance. This involved studying with many distinguished scholars, including Larry Thomas, Nancy Cartwright, Stuart Hampshire, Patrick Suppes, and Anthony Kenny. Your dissertation was on the work of Jean Piaget, with a committee that included Thomas (as chair), Nat Gage, and Julius Moravsick. The thesis also involved study of the work of Lawrence Kohlberg and Carol Gilligan. Your Ph.D., titled *Constructivism as a Basis for a Theory of Teaching*, was awarded in 1973. (I forgot to mention that I was awarded my Ph.D. in the same year.)

After a number of assistant's positions you were to return to Stanford in 1977, becoming a full professor in 1986. I was there for the fall semester of 1981, and we met only briefly. Also there, but as a student, was my future wife, Lynda, whom I did not meet then, but you were her mentor, and a close relationship, both academic and as friends, has ensued. Some philosophy is even done at your Professors' Weekends in September.

Your first book was *Caring: A Feminine Approach to Ethics and Moral Education* (2003a). In the preface to the second edition (2005a) and referring to the first edition, you say:

> Perhaps the greatest contribution of care theory as it is developed here is its emphasis on the caring relation. Relations, not individuals, are ontologically basic, and I use "caring" to describe a certain kind of relation or encounter. . . . Caring is a relationship that contains another, the cared-for, and we have already

suggested that the one-caring and the cared-for are reciprocally dependent. . . . Both play significant parts in caring relations. (Noddings, 2005a, p. xiii)

What interested me in your work from the outset was your use of caring as an ontologically basic *relation*. In the 1980s I was beginning to read Michel Foucault. Of course it was the Foucault of *Discipline and Punish: The Birth of the Prison* (1977), possibly the text most read by educationalists. Why was it read by us? It was hardly because of the logic of relations but, more likely, because it was concerned with power. Power was exercised in schools, referred to by Foucault as *disciplinary blocks* (or blockades). At a seminar on Foucault that I gave in London, Richard Peters asked me what Foucault had said on authority. Not very much, I replied, and to a person who had mentioned power only four times in his famous book—*Ethics and Education* (Peters, 1966). Peters, however, talked much of liberal notions of *authority*.

Foucault had a number of interesting things to say about power, especially "conceptualizing" it as a relation. Unfortunately Foucault used *relation* and *relationship* sometimes as though they were interchangeable terms. You do not, or did not, use *relationship(s)* because of its institutional implications. You not only posit *caring* as being a relation, as is Foucault's account of power, but also it is seen as a fundamental notion for morality because of the starting point of care in the family (the "one-caring" and the "cared-for"). Thus, for you, Nel, morality does not come down written on tablets of stone, from moral principles articulated by philosophers (especially in your case from Kant), or through moral institutions like schools with their principals and principles, and modern business institutions. In effect we "share" Foucault because of his turn to relations. As I remember, your final comment on this topic was "If anything, philosophical morality in the future might retune the relation of caring," and thereby might rescue it from inappropriate use.

Reading recently about caring and the notion of relations, especially with Foucault's various questions and answers to *how* questions and the effects of power, I began to think of his notion of pastoral power, which sometimes seemed to be almost a caring or mentoring type of relation. So I arrived with the example of the Self and the Other, as it featured in the writings of both Simone de Beauvoir and Jean-Paul Sartre. Could it receive a relations exposition? There was a short discussion. You said yes—end of discussion! However I need to say something of what I might have said at Ocean Grove. Here goes, briefly.

In her first novel, *She Came to Stay*, written in 1941 but not published until 1943, Beauvoir explores the concepts of consciousness, mind and body, freedom, authenticity, the existence of the "external" world, and the importance of all of these concepts for the notion of the social Other and the constitution of the Self. I will deal here only with the latter philosophical problem—Self and Other. The central characters are Françoise (Beauvoir), Pierre (Sartre), and Gerbert (Jacques Laurent Bost). She poses the notion, and in opposition to Sartre, that in establishing her Self as a subject, the Other is necessary on both epistemological and ethical grounds (see also *The Blood of Others* and *All Men are Mortal*). At that time Sartre saw the Other as alien, and as a foe to be "overcome." Beauvoir argues that the Other is necessary to assure "her self" that she is a Subject and not merely an Object for the Other.

Gerbert is the necessary Other at the start of the novel and assures Francois that she is indeed a Subject. Subsequently with Pierre they are almost one in her thinking–they are both Subjects (at least for Beauvoir). (It is possible that Sartre stole this version of the Self-Other in *Being and Nothingness* (Sartre, 1958). However, Beauvoir abandons this position to argue that the Other cannot be totally Subjectified, because the Other will be *needed*, if not *objectified* by being used, in their interactions.)

Thus we have two individuals in a relation of caring, or pastoral mentoring, or power, or . . . ? The caring relation has "cared for," mentoring the "mentee," and power "the possibility of resistance" (Foucault, 1996, p. 153). However, the gaze cannot offer such possibilities. Because of the "history" of the Self-Other issue, I believe that it is better suited to a relation-type analysis.

Thank you both for your caring and mentoring over the weekend. Good gardening.

–Jim (James Marshall)

Educating for Happiness

Jack P. Miller

Dear Nel,

I first encountered your work when I read *Caring: A Feminine Approach to Ethics and Moral Education* (2003a) in the mid-1980s. Since then, I have followed your work closely. It has had a profound impact on my own work in holistic education.

Your work is a strong blend of theory and practice. *Caring* was followed by *The Challenge to Care in Schools* (1992), which gives many practical ways that your ideas can be implemented in classrooms. I have cited examples from this text in my own writing, most recently *Educating for Wisdom and Compassion: Creating Conditions for Timeless Learning* (Miller, 2006).

I first met you when we invited you to give the opening keynote speech to first International Conference on Holistic Learning in 1997 at the Ontario Institute for Studies in Education at the University of Toronto. I learned then how you also have been a caring parent with a large family. I am continually amazed how you have been so productive academically while maintaining such strong family and personal commitments.

In 2008 we both keynoted at the Holistic Conference in Guadalajara, Mexico. My talk was followed by yours and you said that although we started from different viewpoints, we agreed about what should happen in education. I had cited the Transcendentalists in my talk and referred to the "divine spark" within each of us. You then said you did not share that belief (I remember too that you said Jack is a "romantic") but we agreed about the ultimate aims of education and how they might be reached in classrooms.

We both share a deep concern about what is happening in education in North America, with its obsession with testing and such a narrow view of curriculum.

Your book *Happiness and Education* is a powerful call for a different approach to teaching and learning. I strongly agree with your statement that

> happiness depends greatly on being free of suffering, and I have argued that it is a mistake to glorify suffering or to suppose that we are ever justified in deliberately inflicting it. It depends, perhaps most importantly, on loving connections with others—intimate relations with a few and cordial cooperative relations with most of those we meet regularly (Noddings, 2003b, p. 73)

In my talk in Mexico I had spoken about love and how we can nurture it in educational settings; we both believe in the centrality of what you call "loving connections."

I was sorry that you were not able to join us in Bhutan because of an illness in your family. As you know, that country has made a commitment to align its education system with the country's goal of "gross national happiness" and we could have benefited greatly from your presence at the conference held in December 2009. Still I am sure your book *Happiness and Education* will be an invaluable support for what they are attempting to do there. It is encouraging how one country is adopting a much more holistic approach to education than we currently see in North America.

You have emphasized the importance of joy in learning and that it "should precede responsibility." How rarely we hear about joy in education, as it seems so out of place in a world of high-stakes testing. The education you propose in your books would lead to more joy in our schools.

Joy is also missing in higher education. Again, I cite from *Happiness and Education*:

> A similar caution is required, however, in conducting discussions on the topics of class, race and gender. A great worry for critical theorists—one that should

receive far more attention than it does at present—is that efforts of critical peda-
gogues induce anger alienation, and hopelessness instead of wisdom and practical action. "Discussion" can deteriorate into venting and blaming thus causing
increased separation among groups. (Noddings, 2003b, p. 104)

What underlies all your work is a deep and abiding humanity that somehow has receded from current educational discourse. Your humanistic vision
is always articulated in a manner that is scholarly and reasoned. In my review of your book *Critical Lessons* for the *British Journal of Educational Studies*
(Miller, 2009) I concluded with this statement.

Overall her writing has provided a comprehensive agenda for education. It is a
vision that is so desperately needed in our age of high stakes testing and obsession with accountability. I hope very much that her writing can penetrate the
current agenda and help us develop a broader dialogue about what our schools
should be doing. (p. 93)

I am sure that this book of letters can contribute significantly to that
dialogue and help move toward the vision that you have articulated and so
many of us share. I also look forward to your continuing contributions to
that dialogue.

With deep gratitude and warmest wishes,

Jack Miller

A Case of Mistaken Identity

Eugene F. Provenzo, Jr.

Dear Nel,

You probably don't remember, but we first met in person in Chicago in
the fall of 1998. We had come to Chicago as part of the Public Project on Religion, sponsored by the University of Chicago and the Pew Memorial Trust.
We met on a Saturday in a hotel at O'Hare airport. About a dozen people
(mostly academics and policy people) came in from around the country. Activists from the Chicago community also participated in the program. I was
excited about finally getting to meet you in person. At that time I had read
your book on care and a couple of your articles. Despite this, I had never
seen a photograph of you and had never seen or met you at a conference.

I suppose this is one of the things that I like and respect most about you—
your "down-to-earthiness," as well as your practicality and your genuineness.
This is not to take away at all from your scholarship, which I know very well

(I believe I have now read almost everything that you have written). But it does seem to me that almost everything you say, except for an occasional diversion into some aspect of traditional philosophy, is profoundly grounded in the practical and real. You understand children and what they need in order to learn. You know how classrooms and schools actually work. I value your insights from having taught high school and elementary school for 20 years and having raised ten children with your equally practical and down-to-earth husband, Jim. Somehow you manage to deal with profound ideas and root them in the practical and the everyday.

Thanks for doing so. Through my reading your work, and knowing you a bit in person, you have made me a better scholar, a more thoughtful person, and a better teacher. Your gifts to the field are many, but perhaps none is more important than the way you constantly remind us, through your writing and your presence in the field, of what it is that actually is important in our work.

—Eugene F. Provenzo, Jr.

University of Miami

"But, Seriously . . ."

Paul Shorc

Dear Nel,

Almost 3 decades have gone by, incredibly, since I sat at the back of your class on curriculum theory at Stanford in the first semester of my doctoral program. What followed is a story that I've told many times to my own students: When the final written examination for the course was handed out, for some reason I decided to "push the envelope" on one of the answers and spent the holiday break sweating over how my professor would react to my answer. When the exam was handed back, there was a note in the margin asking me to come to see you . . . I was truly puzzled (and a little apprehensive) as to what it was all about, but went to your office.

The upshot of this first meeting was a 2-year-long project that was one of the most intellectually exciting experiences of my life, and one that I constantly reflect upon to this very day. But enough about my own experience—here is what *you* did, and why it was and is important.

First, and most impressive, you very skillfully balanced support and encouragement for someone just starting an academic career with thoughtfully expressed—and caring—criticisms of writing and thinking. It turns out that this balance is much harder than it sounds. Every writer, novice or veteran, likes to hear validation of her or his work, but every writer can still benefit from discussion, criticism, and revision. This of course includes the senior partner in such an undertaking. You were even prepared to learn from me, a student, and there was nothing patronizing about your offer. Your sensitive managing of the complex role of mentor/coauthor has influenced my teaching and writing ever since.

Early on, you seized upon the description of the philosophical case that we had to build as "a serious view." It was the perfect description, as well, of how you approached every intellectual problem. There was never a whiff of pomposity or pretension in your approach, but it was completely serious: The questions under consideration were not verbal games or careerist stepping-stones, but important issues that demanded our attention and should be weighed with careful rationality, leavened with the excitement of the chase and a passion for exactitude. The weighing of choices, the assembling of narratives and arguments, the locating of ideas within their cultural contexts, the contemplation of the influence of one thinker upon another: Each of these came to life in memorable, serious ways.

There was something very new and yet very old about this approach. New because here was a woman, neither a traditionalist nor the caricature of the collegiate "radical feminist" of the day, undertaking this quest in an environment that for all its claims to progressive thinking, still harbored deeply sexist attitudes. Simultaneously, you were completing the book that would make you famous and be hailed as an innovator in your interpretation of femininity. But your approach to questions of relation, definition, and theory building had an old and honorable pedigree. It seemed that as we created our own work we were in conversation with men (and yes, they were almost entirely men) from other times and places who had struggled with similar questions. The need for the conversation, and the respect with which it was conducted, were commonalities that stretched back over the centuries. Only later, after I'd seen much more of the fragmentation of academic life, would the extraordinary breadth of the investigation you proposed, and your freedom from the turf war mentality, become really apparent.

In the process, and almost without realizing it, I also gained from you the best training in writing I have ever received.

One hears much in academe about both the alleged "conflict" between teaching and research and, at the same time, a great deal about the importance of teaching and so on. Up close, working with you in your office and at your house, I saw that as you constructed your own academic identity, one based upon how you understood personal integrity and the relation between teacher and student, research and teaching were not simply exercising a truce but were actually in harmony and that this harmony expressed the very philosophical views you were espousing. Again, like the balance between criticism and support of a beginning author, this may sound easy but is far from it. And although we students knew very little about it at the time, you were simultaneously balancing these two concerns with the pressures of our own progress toward tenure. *Humility, resolve,* and *dignity* are some of the words that come to mind when I think of how you proved yourself during those years. You also cooked some great meals when I was over working at your house!

Ultimately I learned a great deal from working with you, even if much of what was of greatest value did not start to sink in for years to come. Today the lessons still seem vitally important even as the university environment has kept changing, with inquiry for its own sake, conversation, and reflection facing even greater challenges than in the early 1980s. The temptations of superficial measures of productivity, of quick fixes to economic woes and the pressures of a texting culture that demands immediate feedback make the sort of tutorial that we undertook increasingly an endangered species. Yet it is an example of just how good a learning experience within a university setting can be.

With gratitude and admiration,

Paul Shore

Legacy in Mentoring

Lynda Stone

Dear Nel,

I have ruminated over this letter because it is much too little to express our relation over the past 25 years. You have been and remain my teacher, my friend, my family. As with so many others in this volume, you are my mentor. Given your continual example of thinking and writing, I have turned to a bit of a scholarly inquiry as a testament to your legacy.

Mentoring, with ancient roots that I will take up subsequently, is commonly mentioned in all aspects of organized social life today. This is especially true in complex institutional settings in which expert and novice persons work together. Everyone identifies at least for a time as "mentor" and "mentee" (where did this come from?). In my school of education, assistant professors have seniors assigned as "formal" mentors; others act informally to offer advice, be sounding boards, help with career development. In precollegiate schools, mentoring programs for probationary teachers are common. Whether "successful" or not, in these situations relationships sometimes become caring relations and perhaps more often they do not. In all, however, something of the mentoring may remain as a legacy.

Your own legacy to me is composed of many aspects. A first is lineage, of which I am proud. Reaching back, there is you, as well as Larry Thomas, who

I did know a little, and John Brubacher. Your husband, Jim, asked me recently about my own students; they are part of a lineage now too. And places like Stanford and UNC Greensboro enhance and foster lineage and legacy. Are we not fortunate? Lineages do contribute to legacy but are never sufficient.

A second aspect is located in actions and meanings of mentoring. As you probably know but I did not until recently, the meaning of *mentoring* reaches back to Homer's *Odyssey* and the character of Mentor. Recall the story: Odysseus, the king of Ithaca, goes off to fight in the Trojan War, leaving his wife, Penelope, and son Telemachus, behind. After many years, Telemachus goes in search of his absent father. As Robert Fagles writes in a recent translation, "[The] prince sat down as Mentor took the floor, Odysseus' friend-in-arms, to whom the king, sailing off to Troy, committed his household, ordering one and all to obey the old man and he would keep things steadfast and secure" (1996, Book 2, stanzas 250–254). From this origin of friend to father and then to son, the *Oxford English Dictionary* defines *mentor* as "adviser or counselor"; a conceptual legacy is born. Also included in the entry is reference to the "best" modern source of meaning, a novel, *The Adventures of Telemachus* by François Salignac de la Methe-Fénelon.

Meaning of mentoring becomes especially interesting in the context of this late 17th-century reinterpretation of the myth. The text I read is an English translation from John Hawkesworth for the Earl of Shaftesbury in the late 18th century in London and republished in New York in the mid-19th century. The reprinted 2010 text is copied (complete with thumb marks) from archives at the University of Michigan. For me, the legacy of great literature is represented in this textual lineage—in what Foucault might name as recurring histories of the present, writings and readings across millennia are each intelligible for their times. Learned from you, in any search for meaning there are always stories to be told, insights to be garnered, shared, and passed forward.

With this in mind, I want to say a bit more about the novel and its author. By Volume 2 of Hawkesworth's translation, two stories converge. In one, Telemachus loans Mentor as a sign of allegiance to the Cretan prince Ideomeneus (later the source of Mozart's opera). The latter is in need of strong guidance and Mentor provides it. The task is to prepare a land for a new people. In the text Mentor speaks and acts on culture, on the military, on trade and agriculture, on social organization. One is reminded in form of *The Republic*. What comes to pass, writes Fénelon, is this: "The mild and equitable government of Idomeneus soon brought the inhabitants of the neighboring crowds . . . to be incorporated with his people and to share the felicity of his reign." The second story returns Mentor to Telemachus as he completes his military operations and heads for home without finding his father. As I read it, the form of the text changes: Mentor speaks but leaves action to the prince himself and a conversation between equals appears to take place. At the close Minerva emerges from the disguise of Mentor and speaks directly to Telemachus; the focus here seems more on the divine than on the practical. She says, "Let the fear of the gods, O Telemachus, be the ruling passion of thy heart: keep it sacred in thy bosom . . . for with this thou shalt possess wisdom and justice, tranquility and joy, unpolluted pleasure, genuine freedom, peaceful affluence, and spotless glory" (Fénelon, 2010, p. 230). With a happy ending, Telemachus does reach Ithaca and finds and recognizes his long-lost father.

On the surface, a legacy of the Greek story seems obvious when retold by Fénelon. In a very complex context that intermingles literature with politics and religion, one learns, moreover, that at least one of Fénelon's purposes is to oppose and criticize the reign of Louis XIV. He may well do this through the character of Mentor and he may hope that a Greek setting disguises his purpose (his efforts fail). But this is a story for another time, one whose own elements might well be enlightening to explore with my own students.

For present purposes, the story of Mentor with his charges offers an opportunity to consider a final aspect of the special legacy of your mentoring. This is to compare mentoring to caring and explore care theory. As indicated above, mentor relationships and engagements, I believe, have a contemporary character. Few would call Mentor's actions on behalf of Idomeneus mentoring—more like meddling, taking too much control. Few too would welcome a Mentor soliloquy on character. First, even though mentoring interactions are typically one to one, to my thinking the source of mentoring differs significantly from caring: a relationship named and bounded rather than a relation enacted and evolving. Second, both may entail caring, but the first typically begins in ethical caring rather than natural. Third, mentoring might well lead to caring, but it does not seem that caring would devolve to mentoring alone. Fourth, both focus on projects of the one mentored, the one cared for, but these projects may well be different in kind: the latter more personal. Finally, intimacy of engrossment of the latter just seems absent in the former. These thoughts are a start.

To close this letter: Homer began a literary and intellectual legacy; Mentor assisted Odysseus and Telemachus in creating their own dynasty and perhaps the legacy of Greek governance.

Nel, in your person and in your work, you have established a legacy, not just of mentoring, but also of caring. We whose lives you have touched are surely richer for this.

Thank you.

Lynda

Shore Education

Stephen J. Thornton

Dear Nel,

I'm writing this to share your philosophy of education with people who may be less familiar with it than I am. It mixes the personal and academic, as I learned most of all from you.

As strange as it may sound, I first fully grasped Nel Noddings's educational philosophy from visiting her on vacation. The first time this happened was August 1985. As was a habit in the Stanford years, she was summering in Ocean Grove, on the Jersey Shore. Ocean Grove is less than an hour from where she grew up.

I'd never been to the Jersey Shore before and I still recall being struck by a bolt of salt air as I crossed the hills from the west. Nel and her husband, Jim, had taken a house for the summer, a block or so back from the beach.

After 5 years at Stanford, I'd been around Nel in a wide assortment of situations. But it was not till Ocean Grove that I saw Nel around the clock. Her daily life is her educational scheme enacted: wandering the seashore, collecting bottle glass, swimming, paperback mysteries, summer evenings on the porch, grandchildren, animals, Grandma, a dissertation delivered by courier from California, cooking, gardening, hot dogs, and casual greetings as neighbors stroll by. Despite a definite air of leisure, this vacation home was far from inactive.

Nel's books and articles can be traced to daily experience as much as to formal intellectual sources. Relationship, the cornerstone of Nel's thinking and living, implies respect for individual interests, that you do your best by knowing your own psychology, by getting done what must be done so as to maximize time for what you relish, to see connections between, for instance, gardens, food, distant culture, local life, the oceans around us, and the ebb and flow of an ever-changing shore. Concepts familiar from her education writings—discovery, choice, connection, motivation, interests, aptitudes, rigor, caring—find daily application in the vacation house. But it is critical application. So, for example, gender equity is interpreted not as bland sameness but as valuing and living difference.

I don't recall anyone commenting during that first visit about what I've just been relating. Nor was there any sign that what was going on was in any way remarkable. It is a short leap from the vacation home, however, to why Nel sees narrow instrumental rationales for education as so incomplete. It is not that such views demand too much, but rather that they so underestimate what it means to educate. So much is missed when education is conceived as ready-made and one-size-fits-all. When, as now, policy makers equate the purpose of education as fostering individual economic "success" and national competitive advantage, schools are set up to fail. By the same token, this scheme neglects what might be answers to what ails schools. Years ago, Alfred North Whitehead confronted the same point head on: He contended that the only solution is workers "who enjoy their work" (1967, p. 44). Along these lines, Nel, with Walt Whitman, sees occupations and earning a livelihood, democracy, and self-realization as intimately interconnected in democratic living. As Whitman wrote, "I hear America singing, the varied carols I hear" (Whitman, 1994, p. 80).

I've been to Ocean Grove countless times since 1985. Nel and I often stroll along the boardwalk. We talk of all things. Some of those things find their way into print but far more is winnowing, refining, thinking through, and coming up with examples that seem true to the world. We pass people with their iPods, and we occasionally muse on why they do not listen to the waves, the gulls, the happy squeals of little children paddling. Geography, history, nature study, mathematics, the fine arts, cooking, mystery novels, travel, plants and animals, friends and colleagues, schools come together. On a walk, for instance, it might be talk of cuisine with olive oil evoking Mediterranean climates and cultures from which it came, life there versus here.

Looking at some of my favorite passages in *Happiness and Education* evokes thoughts of boardwalk conversation (Noddings, 2003b, pp. 253–255): If we agree on key concepts and skills in a subject, does the particular content to teach the subject always matter? What are the things everyone must learn, how should it happen, who decides? How do studies in one subject lead to connections to the next subject (do subjects have boundaries, anyway)? Observation in what types of settings would uncover that children love poring over maps? What would demonstrate that what we teach in schools leads to good citizenship?

Nel finds inspiration in some early lines of Dewey's *The School and Society* (1990): "What the best and wisest parent wants for his own child, that must the community want for all its children" (p. 5). Nel finds it peculiar that even distinguished scholars mistake Dewey's meaning. Dewey is certainly not recommending the same education for all children. Nor is it compatible with his outlook that elites should decide the design of school curriculum for the entire community. Rather, Dewey is looking at the school as a social entity involving the entire community. Moreover, Dewey (and Nel) insist that each child, as he makes clear elsewhere in the same passage, differs in motivation and aptitude. "Any other ideal for our schools is narrow and unlovely," Dewey concludes; "acted upon, it destroys our democracy."

I learned from Nel how a powerful few words can be as the basis of an entire argument. I believe that these words of Dewey's present one entryway to Nel's philosophy of education. In them there is stated or implied an ethic of care, a vindication (even celebration) of individual differences, acclamation of education as a community-wide endeavor, and respect for wisdom and reflection. As in life in general, Nel resists compulsion in education. For example, as a former math teacher she is the first to say that mathematics (or any other school subject) beyond the fundamentals is necessarily good for everyone. Rather, through relation, she would have educators work to elicit from young people what is in them and help guide them to develop what it means for their education and future.

With love,

Steve Thornton

Theory in Practice: Nel Noddings's Mentoring

Susan Verducci

Dear Nel,

I am grateful for this opportunity to express my thoughts about your work in this semiformal and public way. I fear that if I spoke these words aloud to you, a "pshaw" would inevitably escape your lips. Of all the things you introduced me to, the "pshaw" continues to be one of my favorites.

I was living in New York City at the time, retooling my life, when I picked up *The Challenge to Care in Schools* (Noddings, 1992) from a display table in a bookstore. My life's trajectory changed as I discovered a new passion. I applied to Stanford for one reason: to study with you. I wanted to learn to think about the sorts of things you wrote about.

You have been the primary caretaker in my professional life since the first day of school, when I sat, scrubbed and shiny, in your office and asked, "What courses shall I take?" Leaning back in your chair, touching your fingertips together as if in prayer, you responded, "Well, now, what would *you* like to take?" My boat left the dock that day in a moment emblematic of your mentoring and your caring. You were there to help me configure my path, but you weren't going to do it for me. At that moment, the floor vanished beneath me. I was used to treadmill education. Step on. Step off, diploma in hand. Although I'd been educated in the arts, there had been no flexibility in what others thought should constitute my training. Being asked to compose my academic life was new and unnerving.

I was nervous on many fronts. Like you, I discovered philosophy in graduate school, having never taken a course in college. My BFA and MFA in acting prepared me for a world centered on the emotional and physical lives of characters; it did not prepare me for a full-time life of the mind. As my advisor, you had your work cut out for you. Luckily for me, you have been more than up to the task. These are just a few things I learned from you.

"Trust and be patient." That first year, I found myself in a foreign land where people spoke philosophy in sentences like "The epistemology of normative value(s) is always already participating in the legitimation of pedagogical institutions." Everything I read and heard sounded vitally important and at the same time vaguely impenetrable. I felt alone in a sea of ideas expressed in obscuring language. I longed for the relative clarity of Samuel Becket and Harold Pinter. Instead, I got Husserl, at the decipherable rate of one paragraph per hour. I felt unmoored. Adrift. What I couldn't see, but gradually began to feel, that year was that you gently held my boat's rope in your hands. There was usually no tension on that rope, but when the winds of my ignorance and philosophical youth pulled me off course (remember that paper on the evolutionary underpinnings of empathy?) the rope gently became taut. At which point, I began the slow and painful process of righting myself.

Over time, you taught me to trust and be patient with the sort of discomfort I was feeling. You gently assured me it was a sign of impending growth, while at the same time you introduced me to Dewey's notion of disequilibrium. You taught me to trust and be patient with ambiguity, ambivalence, and confusion—that they can be part of the process and the product of good work. You also taught me to trust and be patient with myself—that anything worth knowing or doing requires time.

"Consider everything." An image of your slender wagging finger accompanies this phrase. Yes, you wag your finger; your wrist becomes loose and your index finger begins to trace that up-and-down crescent-moon shape. A Mona Lisa smile appears on your face and you say, "Now, now, wait a minute. Let's look at that more closely." It would drive students nuts, wondering why you would stop to consider the most blatantly wrongheaded of ideas. It would also drive us crazy that you would not commit to taking particular positions in class. I gradually came to realize that you were indeed taking perhaps the most important stance a human and an academic can—an open one. You were willing to consider and mine even the seemingly outlandish for something of value. Instead of telling us what to think, you painstakingly helped us lay out the best version of the ideas and positions under consideration.

Your "consider everything" strategy was also helpful to me in the sense that I often found myself speaking incoherently in class and at conferences—poking around an idea, not fully seeing, understanding, or expressing it. I had solid intuitions, but lacked clarity and words for expression. Other professors would have dismissed my fumblings, but your "consider everything" strategy allowed me the space to tease out the salient points to be developed, even if they were in the end not worth developing. Here, the "confirmation" of care theory—attributing the best possible motive and justification to the cared-for—extended not only to me as a student, but also to ideas, books, and arguments. "First," you oft repeated, "read to believe. Then, read to analyze." In class, when you were unwilling to use your authority to influence our thinking, you were teaching us to be receptive and independent in our work as future professionals. You were teaching us the care and feeding of ideas.

"Philosophy and wine can be mutually enhancing." During my years at Stanford, a small cohort of students, professors, and visiting scholars met at your home every week to discuss philosophical readings outside our regular schoolwork. On these evenings our first order of business was chatting over a glass of wine. We chatted until Jim fled, mumbling about fixing something in the back of the house. From my position on your couch, I learned that thinking happens in collaboration, and that the best thinking can come from being challenged. Of course, Denis Phillips, your longtime friend, colleague, and philosophical foil, was at these gatherings and helpful in this lesson. As I watched you two think (disagree) together, I learned not only that thinking could be a messy road strewn with tricky turns and sudden obstacles but also that philosophy, at its best, is something that is developed and tested in collaborative relationship with others.

Although I had heard the saying that we build knowledge on the shoulders of those who have gone before us, in this forum I came to understand that this manifested in the form of relationships with colleagues as well as relationships with books. Although I can't have a conversation with David Hume, I can have conversations with colleagues about Hume, interactions that push me to think more rigorously and to consider ideas that I otherwise might miss. At times, wine lubricates this process and relaxes rigid notions that inhibit intellectual growth.

"Work and life are not separate." You make this a central theme in your intellectual biography, aptly titled "A Way of Life" (Noddings, 2008). You modeled for me the permeable boundaries between your work and your personal life. I blush to think how many times you and Jim fed me, but you understood and cared about the connection between my developing academic mind, my body, and my soul. You introduced me to your children and grandchildren, to your garden, to the Jersey Shore, and to the importance of having windows that seal properly during a storm. Crawling under your desk in the wee hours of the morning on one of my weekends with you, armed with absorbent towels, I was reminded of my graduate school papers, with their margins decorated in lovely curving question marks gently identifying massive leaks in my thinking. The nearly seamless way that conversation with you weaves the abstractions of philosophy with what is typically considered part of the private domain continues to amaze me. I have memories of grocery shopping with you discussing Bernard Williams, and of talking about the best way to grow beets between sessions at a philosophy conference. This permeability is reflected in the content of your philosophical work as well. It seems to me that one thread through your work is the deconstruction of the way we think of the boundaries between our personal and public lives. *Caring* (2003a), *Educating for Intelligent Belief or Unbelief* (1993), *Starting at Home* (2002), and *Happiness and Education* (2003b) all dismantle the psychological and philosophical walls between the public and the private.

You are a groundbreaking boundary buster. The remarkable paradox is that your "deconstructive" insights and talent seem to have the effect of integration. You draw together your life as a mother with your work as a philosopher. These same books help integrate my life as well. I find myself awakened to places within me that I previously hadn't seen. Once there, I can't stop staring at them—like one of those ambiguous pictures in which a duck becomes apparent in what one thought was a rabbit. Once the rabbit is seen, it takes effort *not* to see the duck. Your work is like that; it is a duck in my rabbit. And viewing both makes me feel I see the world more clearly.

"Attend." One of the most appealing aspects about your philosophical work and your mentoring is that you attend to the real world and real people. Decrying the moral supremacy of "principle" and the false philosophical distinctions between the mind, emotions, and body, you listen to people's inclinations and disinclinations, you attend to their emotional worlds, and you make sense of the educational and moral world in a way that allows its richness, complexity, and ambiguity to be appreciated. In both philosophy and mentoring, you pay receptive attention to the specific reality of others. I never felt like an abstract "student" with you, but always "Susan."

Finally, you taught me to think about "connections." Through your mentoring and scholarship, I have come to believe that schools should cultivate students' abilities to perceive, understand, and make connections in the world, and educators should cultivate a proclivity to act in ways that honor these connections. Connections form the heart of our educational and moral world. They also lie at the heart of your mentoring and your philosophical work.

As I wind down here, my words seem inadequate to the task set before me. Once again, I find myself fumbling with language. You anticipated this; in *Caring* (2003a) you wrote:

> The cared-for glows, grows stronger, and feels not so much that he has been given something as that something has been added to him. And this "something" may be hard to specify. Indeed, for the one-caring and the cared-for in a relationship of genuine caring, there is no felt need on either part to specify what sort of transformation has taken place. (p. 20)

But this does not anticipate my need to express gratitude for your caring. To honor and pay tribute to your ability to live out your philosophical ideas in our relationship is a natural part of what it means to have fully received your acts of care. I am grateful for not only our relationship but also the opportunity to express the "something" you have "added" to me.

In my mind's eye I can see your humble smile, the slight wave of your hand, and your response: "Pshaw."

With love,

Susan Verducci

So Many Footprints . . .

Carol Smith Witherell

Dear Nel,

Where shall I begin? Philosopher, ethicist, feminist, educator, scholar, leader, speaker, colleague, coach, mentor, friend, caregiver/linchpin of an amazing extended family, fellow lover of the ocean–these are all ways that you have touched my life and my teaching over the years.

We first met after a session at the annual meeting of the American Educational Research Association in the mid-1980s. I had attended a session in which you presented a paper on ethics, caring, and the role of dialogue in ethical inquiry. Your presentation enlarged my understanding of ethics in substantial ways, especially with respect to the nature of care and caring, the relational self, circles of caring, the ethical ideal and the ethical self, and reciprocity from a caring perspective. These were important dimensions of ethics that would contribute to my understanding of ethics and moral development in significant ways.

After this session I asked you if you would serve as a discussant for a symposium I was planning on the uses of narrative and dialogue in teaching, counseling, and research, an invitation you kindly accepted. The symposium was accepted for the following year's annual meeting of AERA and was enthusiastically received by a substantial audience. Your discussion was a highlight. The session would serve as the scaffold for a book that you and I edited–*Stories Lives Tell: Narrative and Dialogue in Education,* published in 1991 with contributions from 15 other writers spanning many disciplines. What a pleasure it was to work with you in person and across the miles on this project!

Over the years you also accepted invitations to come to Portland to speak to our Lewis & Clark College Graduate School faculty and students and to the Catlin Gabel and Arbor School communities, generating rich and vibrant dialogue about how schools might live by the ethic of care in their relationships, their dialogue, their curriculum, and their extensions into the community.

Thanks to reading and teaching many of your books and conversations with you when we would get together over the years, I am convinced that caring, fairness and justice, empathy, and imagination are all important strands of moral and ethical development throughout the life span. This enlarged understanding has enhanced my teaching, learning, and writing in so many ways. My students and I increasingly appreciate your claim that models of caring within families and communities should serve as critical scaffolds for social policy. In our graduate school core classes, students in the fields of education and counseling psychology make powerful connections between your writing and their professional practice. They explore in their writings and dialogue circles the ways that caring relations, acts of caring, and authentic dialogue contribute to the formation of healthy individuals, families, and communities.

A school psychology student in one of our graduate core classes wrote the following as his priority professional goal in his professional mission statement at the close of our class:

> Goal 1: Strive to create dialogue between individuals and/or groups in conflict. Understanding comes from experience, interaction, and through encountering and then assimilating the unknown. Creating opportunities for communication, through modeling listening skills, practicing empathy, and finding opportunities for people to come together (individuals, school groups, after-school groups, homes in the community). Appreciation for the "Other" only comes with contact.

Another student who was enrolled in the Master of Arts in Teaching Program wrote about a metaphor from Linda Hogan's *The Woman Who Watches Over the World* that has called her to serve as a facilitator in community building:

> Humans want truth the way water desires to be sea level and moves across the continent for the greater ocean. A droplet of rain, merging with other drops to form a puddle, the puddle filtering into a creek, the creek meandering into a river, the river rushing into the ocean. This movement, this gravity-induced pull to the truth, is inherent in our human experience. With collaboration we can achieve greatness. And I, as a raindrop, can become a puddle, a creek, a river, an ocean. (Hogan, 2001, p. 15)

It is apparent to me that these students have integrated key dimensions of your ethic of caring and inclusion into the way they will serve their schools and communities.

One of our Lewis & Clark faculty members, the cofounder of Encompass Families Institute, and several fellow members of the City Club of Portland joined me in planning and leading a series of six community forums in 2008 titled "Children at the Center: Envisioning Schools, Families, and Communities That Serve Our Youth." Three of our planning team members were admirers of your writings on the ethic of care. At our fifth forum session, one of our groups reported back to the large group of 30 participants the following recommendations in response to a question they dialogued about: *How do I lead a meaningful, fulfilling, and responsible life? How can we prepare children for such a life?*

1. In order to develop ethics and meaning in life, children need inspirational, caring mentors who have experience and knowledge; who are open, positive, and available; who have inspirational stories and hope; and who inspire ethical relationships with the social/cultural and physical world.
2. Children need modeling of ethical behavior; an honored voice in their families and communities; time for reflection; and opportunities for democratic, collective decision making.
3. Children, their families, and their communities need adequate economic support in order for children to thrive in their social, psychological, and ethical development.
4. Children need authentic connection to self and to the world.
5. Results include children and adults who are able to share, empathize, cooperate, care for others, and live creatively and responsibly, with passion and respect for diversity.

These observations and recommendations led to suggestions in our final session that participants connect with schools and community settings, with organizations like Stand for Children and Children First for Oregon, and with our congressmen and -women to put the ethic of care and the health and well-being of children and families in our state and region at the top of the agenda in shaping social policy. It was further suggested that we explore in a future session what it would require for Portland to meet UNICEF's criteria for being a "child-friendly city." I hope you can see the impact that your work has had on educational and civic organizations with which I have been affiliated.

Nel, I feel profoundly grateful for the gifts of friendship and mentoring that you have extended to me over the years. You have left lasting footprints on so many minds, spirits, and hearts, and mine are surely among them. Thank you for these gifts.

> With deep gratitude and care,
> Carol Smith Witherell, Professor Emeritus
> Lewis & Clark College

is fascinating
[In the book
Gilligan, Sally

e, is woven through
the caring relation;
hinking and feeling;
nes,

Lynda Stone

rly clear the
cal way of life, and

ded and abetted by her hus-
at follows is a composite of an
equent visits across her retire-
e, it complements the foreword
er members of the family. The
astic and extremely productive
tegrally facilitated by an overall

ocial work, an im-
tue ethics—a topic

ford University as Lee L. Jacks
ed as associate and acting dean
decade. Since that time she has
d universities, including Teachers
is University of Miami. Among
a few doctorates, election to and
Education, and presidencies of the
John Dewey Society. Beginning in
nclude 8 since 1998, almost 1 each
al appeal is that books have been
range from Arabic to Vietnamese.
ificant number of articles and chap-
Along with a chapter, these publica-
erspersed typically with one or more

o. They care . . .
dents, but they
ent should do,
gy in making
o listen, wants to

irtue ethics, the
s connection of
he "gender fac-
violence and a

ion and expansion of thought is found
Maternal Factor: Two Paths to Morality.

nder care
ot . . . mothers
are more

tle is "Loving
ing to accom-
e dealing with
nnection is to
or discussion
c politics.

the original *Caring* book. A lot has
e of us working in what we now call
he another's work. . . . Someday one

of us ought to write a brief history because it really
to see how each of us came from different roots. . . .
I acknowledge important contributions from Carol
Ruddick, Virginia Held, and Jean Watson].

Their work and others, such as that of Michael Slot
central ideas developed across the text. These include
limitations of obligation, autonomy, and virtue; roles of t
and the conceptual shift from rights to needs. She contin

One of the . . . [aims] was to . . . try to make particula
differences between caring as a way of life, as an ethi
caregiving, which is a set of occupations.

In these occupations such as teaching, nursing, and s
portant distinction has to be made between care and vir
that has concerned Nel in many publications.

Now I wouldn't say, "Well, virtue carers don't care." N
in the sense that they have a deep concern for their stu
are people who usually start out knowing what the stud
be, learn, and so forth, and then they give all their ener
sure that happens. Whereas the relational carer wants t
hear what the student would like to do.

In addition to updating differences between care and v
newest book offers two relatively radical moves. The first i
evolutionary biology. It relates to an avowed emphasis on t
tor." The second, also gendered but male, is a proclivity to
preoccupation with war. Of the first, she relates,

I am not claiming that maternal instinct automatically is
ethics, but there is an evolutionary factor there. You've go
who attend to their infants and respond accordingly, and
likely to have surviving infants.

The second is a preview of her next book. Its working ti
and Hating War." In the interview she describes current read
pany writing. This ranges from tracts on ancient Greece to those
present-day Afghanistan. As in all projects, the significant con
contemporary schooling. For herself and by others, she calls f
about violence and war and patriotism, religion, and democrati

What strikes family, students, friends, and visitors is the integral connection every day of professional and personal life within what Nel calls "structure." First, she employs a list of academic projects and deadlines that is updated once a month. She has kept these yellow-paper lists and through them can chart her career.

> I start a new list for . . . [the month] with what's still left. . . . There's a column for writing and another for speaking. . . . So they are pretty much in order . . . [and] I usually put the deadline in parentheses. . . . It's sitting there for me to look at and make decisions on. . . . [But] one of the things that my husband enjoys so much, and I guess that I do too, is that . . . when you have a job . . . [or retirement] like this, you don't know what's going to happen! An email may come through with a wonderful invitation.

These brief lists also are part of the writing of each presentation, article, chapter, and book. All items are checked off by her in the meticulous hand of a mathematician. In general Nel summarizes her view of structure. Without some organization, she says,

> We get into this guilt, agonizing, "I should be doing this and I should be doing that." I am very rarely troubled by that sort of thing. And in part it's because I am so organized and structured. . . . You know there are people who don't like to be structured but my sense is that I . . . [actually] have more time to relax . . because when you know what's coming up, then you know when you've got free.

One component of free time is reserved for prodigious reading, both for projects and for pleasure.

Moreover, at several points in the recent interview, Nel particularly speaks of "thinking time." It ought, she says, to come naturally, as a normal part of any day.

> Most of the hard work for me goes into that thinking area. . . . A lot of thinking goes on in the wee hours of the morning. . . . Somewhere around 3:00 a.m., 4:00, my mind is awake. I don't necessarily get out of bed but my mind is awake. . . . Laurie loves this. . . . Some days I wake up, checking out to be sure I can still develop the quadratic formula.

Not only does thinking focus on current writing but it also can leap forward to future work. One morning at the breakfast table, for example, Nel hastily scribbled a chapter outline for a book on democracy at the bottom of a grocery list; thinking time is whenever it comes.

Structures exist and operate with "caring" in mind. Nel writes about and lives many aspects of daily caring. For example, at an outdoor family meal, conversation centered around granddaughter Kayla's dilemma over choice in high school courses. How should personal choice balance with college preparation? Prominent in her family life are gardening and cooking, over which she exhibits great care. The Noddings's home in coastal New Jersey is fronted on two sides by gardens, one which produces much of their summer vegetables (and canned goods for winter) and the other which offers spring, summer, and fall flowers of endless variety. Two images stand out: broccoli soup from garden produce and hanging baskets of red geraniums on all porches and decks.

Nel prefers to write in the morning, but especially in summer, watering comes first. This is part of joint organization between her and Jim. She explains that "the week is roughly carved out."

> Jim and I decide ahead of time which day we'll probably do the shopping. . . . [And then when there are local appointments] and when I am planning a morning in the kitchen . . . [to] restock the freezer with good stuff like lentil soup and spaghetti sauce.

Seasonal structures are evident as well. An example is a yearly vegetable garden listing with months and notations of planting and harvesting beans, corn, wonderful Jersey tomatoes. Likewise, next year's seed orders are considered from catalogs and ordered well ahead. One notices, by the way, that Nel's wardrobe is functional and elegant in its straightforward simplicity.

Nel Noddings is flunking retirement! Today she is living what appears to all as a highly satisfying and productive life. With a large family, the complexities of life today, and even the inevitabilities of older life, of course there is no perfection. Overall, however, her continuing facilitation of the structured blending of interests and projects, both professional and personal, can serve as an important lesson for us all.

References

Allport, G. (1955). *Becoming: Basic considerations for a psychology of personality*. New Haven, CT: Yale University Press.

Apffel-Marglin, F., with PRATEC. (Eds.). (1998). *The spirit of regeneration: Andean culture confronting Western notions of development*. London: Zed Books.

Apple, M. W. (1979). *Ideology and curriculum*. Boston: Routledge.

Apple, M. W. (1993). *Official knowledge*. New York: Routledge.

Arendt, H. (1993). *Between past and future*. New York: Penguin Books. (Original work published 1954)

Arnold, R. (2005). *Empathic intelligence: Teaching, learning, relating*. Sydney: University of New South Wales Press.

Au, W. (2010). The idiocy of policy: The anti-democratic curriculum of high-stakes testing. *Critical Education, 1*(1). Available at http://m1.cust.educ.ubc.ca/journal/v1n1

Ayers, W. (2001). *To teach: The journey of a teacher* (2nd ed.). New York: Teachers College Press.

Barone, T. (2001). *Touching eternity: The enduring outcomes of teaching*. New York: Teachers College Press.

Bateson, G. (1972). *Steps to an ecology of mind: Collected essays in anthropology, psychiatry, evolution, and epistemology*. San Francisco: Chandler Publishing Co.

Belenky, M. F., et al. (1997). *Women's ways of knowing: The development of self, voice, and mind* (10th anniversary ed.). New York: Basic Books

Bowlby, J. (1969). *Attachment and loss*. New York: Basic Books.

Browning, R. (1902). *The poetical works of Robert Browning* (A. Birrell, Ed.). New York: Macmillian.

Brubacher, J. (1962). *Modern philosophies of education*. New York: McGraw-Hill.

Buber, M. (1970). *I and thou* (W. Kaufmann, Trans.). New York: Charles Scribner's Sons.

Cahn, S. (2007). *Classic and contemporary readings in the philosophy of education*. Indianapolis, IN: Hackett Publishing.

Cajete, G. (1999). *A people's ecology: Explorations in sustainable living*. Santa Fe, NM: Clear Light.

Callahan, J., & Tuana, N. (2008). *Feminist philosophers: In their own words* [DVD]. University Park, PA: FemPhil Productions.

Cherryholmes, C. H. (1988). *Power and criticism: Poststructural investigations in education.* New York: Teachers College Press.

Chittister, J. (1990). *Job's daughters: Women and power* [Madeleva Lecture in Spirituality]. Mahwah, NJ: Paulist Press.

Collins, P. H. (2000). *Black feminist thought: Knowledge, consciousness, and the politics of empowerment* (2nd ed.). New York: Routledge.

Damasio, A. (1994). *Descartes' error: Emotion, reason, and the human brain.* New York: Grosset/Putnam.

Damasio, A. (2000). *The feeling of what happens: Body, emotion, and the making of consciousness.* London: Vintage.

Damasio, A. (2003). *Looking for Spinoza: Joy, sorrow, and the feeling brain.* Orlando, FL: Harcourt Books.

Dewey, J. (1916). *Democracy and education. An introduction to the philosophy of education.* New York: Free Press.

Dewey, J. (1933). *How we think. A restatement of the relation of reflective thinking to the educative process* (rev. ed.). Boston: D.C. Heath.

Dewey, J. (1989). *Freedom and culture.* Buffalo, NY: Prometheus. (Original work published 1939)

Dewey, J. (1990). *The school and society; and, The child and the curriculum.* Chicago: University of Chicago Press.

Dewey, J., & Bentley, A. (1949). *Knowing and the known.* Boston: Beacon.

Dickinson, E. (1960). *The complete poems of Emily Dickinson* (T. Johnson, Ed.). New York: Little, Brown.

Digiovanni, L. (2005). *Becoming multicultural teachers: An exploration of transformation in white female elementary educators.* Available at http://www.georgiasouthern.edu/etd/archive/Fall2005/ldigiova/digiovanni_lee_w_200501 _edd.pdf

Eisler, R. (2000). *Tomorrow's children: A blueprint for partnership education in the 21st century.* Boulder, CO: Westview Press.

Eisler, R., & Miller, R. (Eds.). (2004). *Educating for a culture of peace.* Portsmouth, NH: Heinemann.

Esteva, G., & Prakash, M. S. (1998). *Grassroots postmodernism: Remaking the soil of cultures.* London: Zed Books.

Farina, R. (1966). Children of darkness [recorded by Joan Baez]. On *Joan* [vinyl recording]. New York: Vanguard.

Fénelon, S. (2010). *The adventures of Telemachus, the son of Ulysses* (J. Hawkesworth, Trans.). New York: Leavitt-Trow. (Original work published 1699)

Foucault, M. (1977). *Discipline and punish: The birth of the prison* (A. Sheridan, Trans.). New York: Vintage.

Foucault, M. (1996). The end of the monarchy of sex. In S. Lotringer (Ed.), *Foucault live: Interviews 1966–84* (pp. 214–225). New York: Semiotext.

Freire, P. (1981). *Education for critical consciousness.* New York: Continuum.

Freire, P. (2007). *Pedagogy of the oppressed.* New York: Continuum. (Original work published 1970)

Giddings, P. J. (1984). *When and where I enter: The impact of Black women on race and sex in America.* New York: William Morrow.

Gilligan, C. (1982). *In a different voice: Psychological theory and women's development.* Cambridge, MA: Harvard University Press.

Giroux, H. (2007). *The university in chains: Confronting the military-industrial-academic complex.* Boulder, CO: Paradigm Publishers.

Glaser, W. (1984). *Control theory.* New York: Harper & Row.

Greene, M. (1988). *The dialectic of freedom.* New York: Teachers College Press.

He, M. F. (2003). *A river forever flowing: Cross-cultural lives and identities in the multicultural landscape.* Greenwich, CT: Information Age Publishing.

He, M. F., & Phillion, J. (Series Eds.). (2008). *Research for social justice: Personal, passionate, participatory inquiries* (The teaching and research for social justice series, Vol. 1). Greenwich, CT: Information Age.

Heidegger, M. (1962). *Being and time* (J. Macquarrie & E. Robinson, Trans.). San Francisco: Harper & Row. (Original work published 1927)

Henderson, J. G., & Kesson, K. R. (Eds.). (1999). *Understanding democratic curriculum leadership.* New York: Teachers College Press.

Henderson, J. G., & Kesson, K. R. (2004). *Curriculum wisdom: Educational decisions in democratic societies.* Upper Saddle River, NJ: Merrill/Prentice Hall.

Hogan, L. (2001). *The woman who watches over the world.* New York: W. W. Norton.

Homer. (1996). *The Odyssey* (R. Fagles, Trans.). New York: Penguin.

Hostetler, K. D. (1997). *Ethical judgment in teaching.* Needham Heights, MA: Allyn & Bacon.

Igoa, C. (1995). *The inner world of the immigrant child.* New York: Routledge.

King, M. L., Jr. (1963). *The strength to love.* Philadelphia: Fortress Press.

Kozol, J. (1992). *Savage inequalities: Children in America's schools.* New York: HarperPerennial.

Kozol, J. (2005). *The shame of the nation: The restoration of Apartheid schooling in America.* New York: Crown Books.

Kozol, J. (2008). *Letters to a young teacher.* New York: Random House.

Kress, T. M. (2010). Tilting the machine: A critique of one teacher's attempts at using art forms to create postformal, democratic learning environments. *The Journal of Educational Controversy, 5*(1). Available at http://www.wce.wwu.edu/Resources/CEP/eJournal/v005n001/a008.shtml

Lakoff, G., & Johnson, M. (2003). *Metaphors we live by.* Chicago: University of Chicago Press. (Original work published 1980)

Martusewicz, R., & Edmundson, J. (2005). Social foundations as pedagogies of responsibilities and eco-ethical commitment. In D. Butin (Ed.), *Teaching context: A primer for the social foundations of education classroom* (pp. 71–92). Mahwah, NJ: Lawrence Erlbaum.

McLaren, P. (2007). *Life in schools: An introduction to critical pedagogy in the foundations of education* (5th ed.). Boston: Allyn & Bacon.

Miller, J. P. (2006). *Educating for wisdom and compassion: Creating conditions for timeless learning.* Thousand Oaks, CA: Corwin Press.

Miller, J. P. (2009, March). Review of Nel Noddings: Critical Lessons: What Our Schools Should Teach. *British Journal of Educational Studies, 57,* 91–93.

Modell, A. (2003). *Imagination and the meaningful brain.* Boston: MIT Press.

Morrison, T. (2008). *What moves at the margin.* Jackson: University of Mississippi Press.

Mother Teresa. (2007). *Mother Teresa: Essential writings.* Maryknoll, NY: Orbis Books.

National Commission on Excellence in Education. (1983). *A nation at risk.* Washington, DC: Author.

Nelson, M. (Ed.). (2008). *Original instructions: Indigenous teachings for a sustainable future.* Rochester, VT: Bear.

Noddings, N. (1981). Caring. *Journal of Curriculum Theorizing, 3*(2), 139–148.

Noddings, N. (1984). *Caring: A feminine approach to ethics and moral education.* Berkeley: University of California Press.

Noddings, N. (1986). Fidelity in teaching, teacher education, and research for teaching. *Harvard Educational Review, 56*(4), 496–510.

Noddings, N. (1989). *Women and evil.* Berkeley: University of California Press.

Noddings, N. (1992). *The challenge to care in schools: An alternative approach to education.* New York: Teachers College Press.

Noddings, N. (1993). *Educating for intelligent belief or unbelief.* New York: Teachers College Press.

Noddings, N. (1995). Teaching themes of care. *Phi Delta Kappan, 76*(9), 675–679.

Noddings, N. (1998a). *Philosophy of education.* Boulder, CO: Westview Press.

Noddings, N. (1998b). Care and moral education. In H. S. Shapiro & D. E. Purpel (Eds.), *Critical and social issues in American education: Transformation in a postmodern world* (pp. 309–320). Mahwah, NJ: Lawrence Erlbaum Associates.

Noddings, N. (2002). *Starting at home: Caring and social policy.* Berkeley: University of California Press.

Noddings, N. (2003a). *Caring: A feminine approach to ethics and moral education.* Berkeley: University of California Press. (Original work published 1984)

Noddings, N. (2003b). *Happiness and education.* New York: Cambridge University Press.

Noddings, N. (2005a). *Caring: A feminine approach to ethics and moral education* (2nd ed.). Berkeley: University of California Press.

Noddings, N. (2005b). *Caring in education: The encyclopedia of informal education.* Available at http://www.infed.org/biblio/noddings_caring_in_education.htm

Noddings, N. (2005c). *The challenge to care in schools: An alternative approach to education* (2nd ed.). New York: Teachers College Press.

Noddings, N. (Ed.). (2005d). *Educating citizens for global awareness.* New York: Teachers College Press.

Noddings, N. (2005e). On community. *Educational Theory, 46*(3), 245–268.

Noddings, N. (2006a). *Critical lessons: What our schools should teach.* New York: Cambridge University Press.

Noddings, N. (2006b). A morally defensible mission for schools in the 21st century. In E. Provenzo (Ed.), *Critical issues in education: An anthology of readings* (pp. 39–48). Thousand Oaks, CA: Sage.

Noddings, N. (2007). *When school reform goes wrong.* New York: Teachers College Press.

Noddings, N. (2008). A way of life. In L. J. Waks (Ed.), *Leaders in philosophy of education: Intellectual self-portraits* (pp. 135–144). Rotterdam, The Netherlands: Sense Publishers.

Noddings, N. (2010). *The maternal factor: Two paths to morality.* Berkeley: University of California Press.

Noddings, N., & Shore, P. (1984). *Awakening the inner eye: Intuition in education.* New York: Teachers College Press.

Noddings, N., & Yu, T. (2004, May 12). Learning to care in an uncaring time. *China Reading Weekly,* p. 41. [Published in Chinese]

Nussbaum, M. (1997). *Cultivating humanity: A classical defense of reform in liberal education.* Cambridge, MA: Harvard University Press.

O'Toole, K. (1998, February 4). Noddings: To know what matters to you, observe your actions. *Stanford Online Report.* Available at http://newsservice.stanford.edu/news/1998/february4/noddings.html

Palmer, P. (1997). *The courage to teach: Exploring the inner landscape of a teacher's life.* San Francisco: Jossey-Bass.

Peters, R. S. (1966). *Ethics and education.* London: Allen & Unwin.

Pinar, W. F. (Ed.). (1999). *Contemporary curriculum discourses: Twenty years of JCT.* New York: Peter Lang.

Pinar, W. F. (2009). The unaddressed "I" of ideology critique. *Power and Education, 1*(2), 189–200.

Pinar, W. F. (2011). *What is curriculum theory?* (2nd ed.) New York: Routledge.

Pinar, W. F., & Grumet, M. R. (1976). *Toward a poor curriculum.* Dubuque, IA: Kendall-Hunt.

Plato. (1925). Epistle X, in I. A. Post, *Thirteen Epistles of Plato.* Oxford UK: Clarendon Press.

Poplin, M. (1999). The global classroom of the 21st century: Lessons from Mother Teresa and imperatives from Columbine. *Education Horizons, 78*(1), 30–38.

Rasheed, S. (2006). *An existentialist curriculum of action: Creating a language of freedom and possibility.* Lanham, MD: University Press of America.

Reynolds, W. M. (2003). *Curriculum: A river runs through it.* New York: Peter Lang.

Rosenblatt, L. (1978). *Literature as exploration.* New York: Appleton-Century-Crofts. (Original work published 1938)

Roseboro, D. L., & Ross, S. N. (2009). Care-sickness: Black women educators, care theory, and a hermeneutic of suspicion. *Educational Foundations, 23*(3-4), 19–40.

Ryle, G. (2002). *The concept of mind* (3rd ed.). Chicago: University of Chicago Press.

Sameshima, P., & Leggo, C. (2010). The poet's corpus in love: Passionate pedagogy. *Journal of Curriculum Theorizing, 26*(1), 65–81.

Sartre, J. P. (1958). *Being and nothingness: An essay on phenomenological ontology* (E. H. Barnes, Trans.). London: Methuen.

Schubert, W. (1991). Teacher lore: A basis for understanding praxis. In C. Witherell & N. Noddings (Eds.), *Stories lives tell* (pp. 207–233). New York: Teachers College Press.

Schubert, W. H., & Ayers, W. (Eds.). (1992). *Teacher lore: Learning from our own experience.* White Plains, NY: Longman.

Schubert, W. H. (2009). *Love, justice and education: John Dewey and the utopians.* Charlotte, NC: Information Age Publishers.

Schwab, J. (1971). The practical: Arts of eclectic. *School Review, 79,* 493–543.

Slote, M. (2007). *The ethics of care and empathy.* London: Routledge.

Smith, G., & Williams, D. (1999). (Eds.). *Ecological education in action: On weaving education, culture, and the environment.* Albany: State University of New York Press.

Steinberg, S., & Kincheloe, J. (1997). *Kinderculture: The corporate construction of childhood* (2nd ed.). New York: Westview Press.

Stern, D. (1985). *The interpersonal world of the infant.* New York: Basic Books.

Thomas, P. L., & Kincheloe, J. L. (2006). *Reading, writing, and thinking: The post-formal basics.* Rotterdam: Sense.

Townshend, P. (1969). Pinball wizard. On *Tommy* [Record]. Track 13. Los Angeles: Geffen.

Walker, V. S., & Snarey, J. R. (Eds.). (2004). *Race-ing moral formation: African American perspectives on care and justice.* New York: Teachers College Press.

Whitehead, A. N. (1967). *The aims of education and other essays.* New York: Free Press.

Whitman, W. (1994). I hear America singing. In L. B. Hopkins & P. Fiore (Eds.), *Hand in hand: An American history through poetry.* New York: Simon and Schuster.

Williams, B. (1981). *Moral luck: Philosophical papers, 1973–1980.* Cambridge, England: Cambridge University Press.

Witherell, C. S., & Noddings, N. (Eds.). (1991). *Stories lives tell: Narrative and dia-logue in education.* New York: Teachers College Press.

Winnicott, D. (1971). *Playing and reality.* London: Tavistock.

Wolf, B. (2001, November 21). Participants "SEED" diversity on campus. *UW Wisconsin-Madison News.* Available at http://www.news.wisc.edu/6828

Woolf, V. (1963). *Three Guineas.* New York: Harcourt, Brace & Co.

Woolf, V. (1980). *Leave the letters 'til we're dead: Letters of Virginia Woolf (Vol. 6, 1936–1941)* (N. Nicolson & J. Trautman, Eds.). New York: Harcourt Brace Jovanovich.

Yu, T. (2004). *In the name of morality: Character education and political control.* New York: Peter Lang.

Ziarek, E. P. (2001). *An ethics of dissensus: Postmodernity, feminism, and the politics of radical democracy.* Stanford: Stanford University Press.

About the Contributors

Roslyn Arnold is an honorary professor in the faculty of education and social work at the University of Sydney. She has also been dean of education at the University of Tasmania. Her publications include *Mirror the Wind* (a selection of poems) and *Empathic Intelligence: Teaching, Learning, Relating.*

David C. Berliner is Regents' Professor of Education at Arizona State University. Like Professor Noddings he is a member of the National Academy of Education, and he has also served as president of the American Educational Research Association. His academic interests are in the study of teaching and design of educational policy.

Lawrence Blum is Distinguished Professor of Liberal Arts and Education, and professor of philosophy, at the University of Massachusetts, Boston. He works in the area of race studies, multiculturalism, moral philosophy, philosophy of education, and moral education. He is the author of *"I'm Not a Racist, But": The Moral Quandary of Race* (2002) and *"They're Insulting All the White People": High School Kids and Race* (2012).

Liora Bresler is a professor at the University of Illinois, Champaign. She is co-founder of the *International Journal of Education and the Arts*. She has published over 100 papers and books on the arts in education, including the *International Handbook of Research in Arts Education* (2007). Her work has been translated into German, French, Portuguese, Spanish, Hebrew, Finnish, and Chinese.

Laurie Noddings Brooks is the retired chief risk officer of Public Service Enterprise Group. She serves on the boards of The Provident Bank of New Jersey, the NACD NJ Chapter, and Saint Philip's Academy in Newark, NJ. She and her husband Donald have seven children and four grandchildren. Brooks has an M.S. degrees from Carnegie Mellon University in Computational Finance and Stanford University in Petroleum Engineering, and an M.A. and B.A. in mathematics from the University of Colorado. She also has a master's degree in Secondary Education from Duquesne University in Pittsburgh, Pennsylvania, and has taught 7th- and 8th-grade math and science, as well as college-level math courses.

Nicholas C. Burbules is the Gutgsell Professor in the Department of Educational Policy Studies at the University of Illinois, Urbana-Champaign. His primary research focuses on philosophy of education, teaching though dialogue, and technology and education. His most recent book is *Showing and Doing: Wittgenstein as a Pedagogical Philosopher*, coauthored with Michael Peters and Paul Smeyers (2008). He is also currently the editor of *Educational Theory*.

Chris Liska Carger is a professor at Northern Illinois University, where she teaches in the literacy education department. She is a past recipient of the International Reading Association's Arbuthnot Award for Excellence in the Teaching of Children's Literature. Her most recent book is *Dreams Deferred: Dropping Out and Struggling Forward*.

Rachel Lake Chapman graduated from the College of St. Rose in 1996 and received her master's degree in elementary education from the State University of New York, Cortland in 2001. She is an elementary school teacher at heart, but is currently employed by Agnes Scott College as part-time instructor in education.

Daniel Chard is a lifetime resident of South Jersey where he teaches at Rowan University. He received a BFA from the University of South Dakota and a doctorate from Teachers College. Daniel exhibits his landscape paintings regularly at the O K Harris Gallery in New York City.

Pradeep A. Dhillon's research straddles philosophy of language (both analytic and Continental) and mind, aesthetics, and international education. Currently, she is working on a manuscript on aesthetics and philosophy of language for MIT Press. She is the editor for the *Journal of Aesthetic Education.*

Ann Diller is a professor at the University of New Hampshire, where she teaches philosophy of education and works with Ph.D. students. She coauthored *The Gender Question in Education*; her published essays include "Facing the Torpedo Fish." Professor Diller lives on a short mountain in southern New Hampshire.

Riane Eisler is best known for her bestseller *The Chalice and the Blade*. She is also the author of an award-winning book on education, *Tomorrow's Children*, and, most recently, of *The Real Wealth of Nations*. She is president of the Center for Partnership Studies and has received many honors, including the Distinguished Peace Leadership award, earlier awarded to the Dalai Lama.

David Flinders is professor in the School of Education at Indiana University, Bloomington. He is a former AERA vice president for Division B: Curriculum Studies and has served as president of the American Association for Teaching and Curriculum. His interests include curriculum theory, secondary education reform, and qualitative research methods.

Jim Garrison is a professor of philosophy of education at Virginia Tech in Blacksburg, Virginia. His awards include the Scholarly Achievement Award from the Institute of Oriental Philosophy, the John Dewey Society Outstanding Achievement Award, and the Medal of Highest Honor from Soka University in Japan. He is a past president of the Philosophy of Education Society as well as the John Dewey Society.

Marlynn Griffin is professor of educational psychology at Georgia Southern University, with earned degrees in instructional design and educational psychology from Florida State University. Her research interests include social networking, classroom assessment, and teacher education. Her hobbies include watching her children play ball, reading, and traveling.

Madeleine Grumet is a professor of education and communication studies at the University of North Carolina, and former dean of its School of Education. A curriculum theorist specializing in arts and humanities curriculum, she interprets curriculum and teaching through the lenses of feminism, psychoanalysis, and the arts. She is the author of *Bitter Milk: Women and Teaching*, a study of gender and the relationship of teaching and curriculum to experiences of reproduction.

James Henderson is a professor of curriculum studies in the School of Teaching, Learning and Curriculum Studies at Kent State University. His research activities and publications address democratic curriculum leadership and its implications for educational transformation, artistry, and professional development. He is coeditor of the *Journal of Curriculum and Pedagogy*.

Barbara Houston is a professor of education at the University of New Hampshire. Her areas of interest are feminist ethics, moral education, epistemology, and philosophy of education. She is coauthor of the book *The Gender Question in Education: Theory, Pedagogy, and Politics* and has published in numerous journals, including *Hypatia*.

Kathy Hytten is a professor in the Department of Educational Administration and Higher Education at Southern Illinois University, Carbondale. Her specialty areas include philosophy of education, diversity, cultural studies, social justice, and critical pedagogy. She is the 2008–2009 president of the American Educational Studies Association.

Cristina Igoa is a teacher in sheltered English instruction for the Hayward (California) Unified School District, an adjunct professor at Notre Dame de Namur University (Belmont, California), and a director of teacher education in the Oxford Symposium in School-Based Family Counseling. She is the author of *The Inner World of the Immigrant Child* (1995) and "Art as a Second Language" (in *The Invisible Children of Our Society and Schools,* 2007).

Kathleen Kesson is professor of teaching and learning at the Brooklyn Campus of Long Island University. She is coauthor, with James Henderson, of *Curriculum Wisdom: Educational Decisions in Democratic Societies* (2004) and *Understanding Democratic Curriculum Leadership* (1999), and editor, with Wayne Ross, of *Defending Public Schools: Teaching for a Democratic Society* (2004).

Eva Feder Kittay is professor of philosophy, Women's Studies affiliate, and senior fellow of the Center for Medical Humanities, Bioethics and Compassionate Care at Stony Brook University, New York. Her published works include *Love's Labor: Essays on Women, Equality, and Dependency* (1998), *The Blackwell Guide to Feminist Philosophy* (co-edited with Linda Martín Alcoff, 2006), *The Subject of Care: Feminist Perspectives on Dependency* (with Ellen K. Feder, 2003), and *Metaphor: Its Cognitive Force and Linguistic Structure* (1990). She is also the mother of a cognitively disabled woman.

Tricia M. Kress is an assistant professor in the Leadership in Urban Schools doctoral program at the University of Massachusetts, Boston. Her research involves exploring the potential of critical pedagogy and critical research for transformative learning and social change.

Robert Lake is an assistant professor at Georgia Southern University and teaches undergraduate and graduate courses in multicultural education from both a local and global perspective. He is the editor *of Dear Maxine: Letters from the Unfinished Conversation with Maxine Greene* (Teachers College Press, 2010) and author *of Vygotsky on Education* in the Peter Lang Primer Series.

Megan J. Laverty is associate professor in the Philosophy and Education Program at Teachers College, Columbia University, where she teaches courses in the master's and doctorate programs. She is a fellow of the Institute for the Advancement of Philosophy for Children (IAPC) and Reviews Editor for *Thinking: The Philosophy for Children Journal.* She has published a number of articles in international journals of educational philosophy, is the author of *Iris Murdoch's Ethics: A Consideration of Her Romantic Vision,* and is the co-editor of *Playing with Ideas: Modern and Contemporary Philosophies of Education.* She has presented at conferences and seminars in Australia, Brazil, Bulgaria, Canada, Denmark, France, Mexico, Ukraine, the United States, and South Korea.

David Loye, psychologist and evolutionary systems scientist, is the author of the national award-winning *The Healing of a Nation,* a new six-book Darwin Anniversary Cycle, including *Darwin's Lost Theory,* and the forthcoming *Darwin's Second Revolution,* first of the trilogy *Darwin and the Battle for Human Survival.*

James D. Marshall is professor emeritus and former dean, University of Auckland, and research professor, University of North Carolina at Chapel Hill. With a specialty in philosophy of education, he is twice president of the Australasia Philosophy of Education Society and internationally recognized author of numerous books and other publications.

Rebecca Martusewicz, Ed.D., has been a teacher educator at Eastern Michigan University for 22 years, teaching courses that integrate ecojustice content into social foundations courses. She is the director of the Southeast Michigan Stewardship Coalition, working to develop ecojustice education in schools. She is editor and cofounder of *The EcoJustice Review: Educating for the Commons,* an internationally juried online journal, and *Educational Studies: Journal of AESA.*

Susan Jean Mayer is a learning and curriculum theorist who focuses on the pedagogical implications of developmental, cultural, and individual diversity for democratic classrooms. Her research explores the construction of shared understandings. Susan lectures at Brandeis and Northeastern and is writing a book on the distribution of interpretive authority in schools.

Jennifer L. Milam is an assistant professor at the University of Akron in Early Childhood Teacher Education and Curriculum. Jennifer's primary research interests include curriculum and cultural studies at the intersections of race and ethnicity in teaching, learning, and teacher education.

John (Jack) P. Miller is a professor in the department of Curriculum, Teaching, and Learning at the University of Toronto. He is author of more than a dozen books in the field of holistic education and contemplative education.

His latest book, *Whole Child Education*, is being published this year by University of Toronto Press.

Bruce Novak is currently director of educational projects for the Foundation for Ethics and Meaning. His 20-year teaching career has given him a wide range of experiences: teaching English and Social Studies, grades 6–12, in diverse settings in and around Chicago; assisting the English Education program at the University of Chicago; and teaching Psychoanalysis and Education for DePaul University and the Chicago Institute for Psychoanalysis, Humanities and Social Science Core courses at the University of Chicago, Writing at the University of Chicago and Truman College, and Philosophy and Foundations of Education at the University of Chicago and Northern Illinois University.

Denis C. Phillips is professor emeritus of education and philosophy at Stanford University, where he also served as associate and interim dean of the School of Education. A past president of the Philosophy of Education Society, he is also a member of the U.S. National Academy of Education. He moved to Stanford from Australia in 1974.

Eugene F. Provenzo, Jr. is a professor in the Social and Cultural Foundations of Education at the University of Miami. He is the author of a wide range of books in history, education, technology, and cultural studies. Most recently he has served as the editor in chief of *The Sage Encyclopedia of the Social and Cultural Foundations of Education*.

Molly Quinn is associate professor in curriculum studies at Teachers College, Columbia University, New York. She is the author of *Going Out, Not Knowing Whither: Education, the Upward Journey and the Faith of Reason* (2001). Much of her scholarship engages spiritual and philosophical criticism toward embracing a vision of education that cultivates wholeness, beauty, compassion, and social action.

Shaireen Rasheed is an associate professor of philosophy in the School of Education at Long Island University. Currently she is working on a manuscript that focuses on creating a phenomenological ethics when discussing issues of a sexualized Muslim women's identity within a post-colonial context. Her other books include *An Existentialist Curriculum of Action*, in which she explores the relationship of aesthetic education and critical thinking in the work of Maxine Greene.

William Reynolds teaches in the Department of Curriculum, Foundations and Reading at Georgia Southern University. His two most recent books are

Expanding Curriculum Theory: Dis/positions and Lines of Flight (2004) and *The Civic Gospel: A Political Cartography of Christianity* (2009).

Sabrina Ross is an assistant professor of curriculum studies at Georgia Southern University. She received her Ph.D. in curriculum and teaching with a specialization in cultural studies from the University of North Carolina at Greensboro. Her scholarly interests include race/ethnic and gender identities, critical pedagogy, and philosophies of education.

Sara Ruddick taught philosophy at the New School of Social Research. She is author or editor of a number of books including *Maternal Thinking: Towards a Politics of Peace*. Ruddick is most famous for her analysis of the practices of thinking and epistemological perspective that emerges from the care of children. She argues that mothering is a conscious activity that calls for choices, daily decisions, and a continuing, alert reflectiveness.

Pauline Sameshima's work centers on curriculum, arts and technology integration, collaborative and creative scholarship, ecoresponsive pedagogies, and innovative forms of knowledge production and acknowledgment. Her books include *Seeing Red, Climbing the Ladder with Gabriel* (with Roxanne Vandermause, Stephen Chalmers, and Gabriel), and *Poetic Inquiry* (with Monica Prendergast and Carl Leggo).

William H. Schubert is professor of education and coordinator of the Graduate Curriculum Studies Programs at the University of Illinois at Chicago.

Paul Shore has held teaching and research appointments at Saint Louis University; the University of Wrocław, Poland, Charles University, Prague; Harvard Divinity School; the University of Edinburgh; and Collegium Budapest and most recently, in the faculty of history at the University of Cambridge.

Shilpi Sinha is an assistant professor in the Department of Curriculum and Instruction at Adelphi University, Garden City, New York, where she teaches courses in the philosophical foundations of education. Her research interests include ethical encounters with otherness, postmodern and postcolonial thought, multicultural education, and philosophy of education.

Barbara Stengel is professor of the practice of education at Vanderbilt University's Peabody College, where she also serves as director of secondary education. She has a longtime interest in the moral and relational dimensions of teaching, learning, and leadership. Her current research focus is emotion, especially fear, in teaching/learning interaction.

Lynda Stone is professor of philosophy of education, director of graduate studies, and area chair of Culture, Curriculum and Change (CCC) at the University of North Carolina at Chapel Hill. She teaches courses in the Ph.D. program in education, CCCs, and the Master of Arts in Teaching programs. She is also the current president of the John Dewey Society.

Barbara Thayer-Bacon, Ph.D. (Indiana University, Bloomington), professor, teaches graduate courses on philosophy and history of education, social philosophy, and cultural diversity at the University of Tennessee. Her primary areas of scholarship as a philosopher of education are feminist theory and pedagogy, pragmatism, and cultural studies in education.

Stephen J. Thornton is professor and chair of the Department of Secondary Education at the University of South Florida. His books include *Teaching Social Studies That Matters*, *The Curriculum Studies Reader* (with David Flinders), and *Teaching Social Studies to English Language Learners* (with Barbara Cruz).

Susan Verducci is a professor of humanities and coordinator of an undergraduate teacher preparation program at San José State University. She co-edited *Democracy, Education and the Moral Life* (2009) and *Taking Philanthropy Seriously: Beyond Noble Intentions to Responsible Giving* (2006). Her fields of interest include educational philosophy, ethics, moral development, philanthropy, and professional education.

Dilafruz Williams is professor of educational leadership and policy, Portland State University. Her academic scholarship and activism intersect. She is cofounder of the Sunnyside Environmental School and Learning Gardens Laboratory.

Carol Smith Witherell is professor emeritus at the Graduate School of Education and Counseling Psychology, Lewis & Clark College in Portland, Oregon. Her specialties are ethics and moral education, child development and learning, and uses of narrative and dialogue in exploring intercultural and gender themes.

Tianlong Yu is an associate professor of education at Southern Illinois University Edwardsville. Born and raised in China and educated in both China and the United States, Yu teaches and writes on the social foundations of education, with a keen interest in the social and political issues around moral education.